WASHBURN

EXTRAORDINARY ADVENTURES
OF A YOUNG MOUNTAINEER

WASHBURN

EXTRAORDINARY ADVENTURES
OF A YOUNG MOUNTAINEER

Among the Alps with Bradford
Bradford on Mount Washington
Bradford on Mount Fairweather

BRADFORD WASHBURN
FOREWORD BY DAVID ROBERTS

Appalachian Mountain Club Books
Boston, Massachusetts

Front and back cover photographs: © Bradford Washburn, courtesy of
Panopticon Galleries, Waltham, MA
Cover design: Mac & Dent
Book design: Kristin Sperber
Interior images scanned by Panopticon Galleries, Waltham, MA.

Washburn: Extraordinary Adventures of a Young Mountaineer
© 2004 by Appalachian Mountain Club. All rights reserved.

Distributed by The Globe Pequot Press, Inc., Guildford, CT.

Among the Alps with Bradford ©1927 by G. P. Putnam's Sons, New York.
Bradford on Mount Washington ©1928 by G. P. Putnam's Sons, New York.
Bradford on Mount Fairweather ©1930 by G. P. Putnam's Sons, New York.

Washburn, Bradford, 1910–
Washburn : extraordinary adventures of a young mountaineer among the Alps
with Bradford, Bradford on Mount Washington, Bradford on Mount
Fairweather/Bradford Washburn ; foreword by David Roberts.
p. cm.
ISBN 1-929173-72-5 (alk. paper)
1. Washburn, Bradford, 1910– 2. Mountaineers—United States—Biography. I.
Title.
GV199.92.W35A34 2004
796.52'2'092—dc22
2004012924

The paper used in this publication meets the minimum requirements of the
American National Standard for Information Sciences—Permanence of Paper
for Printed Library Materials, ANSI Z39.48-1984.∞

Printed on recycled paper using soy-based inks. ⊕
Printed at Versa Press in the United States of America.

10 9 8 7 6 5 4 3 2 1   04 05 06 07 08 09

CONTENTS

FOREWORD

It is a delight to be able to salute a man, still hale and hearty at the age of 94, by pointing out that he was always a precocious fellow. Although Brad Washburn would go on from his teenage years to become the greatest mountaineer in Alaskan history, as well as arguably (along with Vittorio Sella) one of the two finest mountain photographers ever, he had, by the age of twenty, published four books. Yes, four: for he had preceded the three adventure yarns reprinted in this volume with a guidebook called *Trails and Peaks of the Presidential Range*, privately printed by his uncle when Brad was sixteen.

Of course, Brad was precocious as a mountaineer, as well as as an author. The White Mountains were his first love: he reached the top of New England's highest peak, Mount Washington, at the age of eleven, then, four years later, in the company of his father and brother, made his first winter ascent of the deceptively dangerous mountain. But it was in the Alps, to which he was introduced in 1926, at the age of sixteen, that he first made a lasting mark. That summer he bagged three of Europe's giant peaks: Mont Blanc, Monte Rosa, and the Matterhorn. The next year, in the tow of expert Chamonix guides—during the season chronicled in *Among the Alps with Bradford*—he made his first significant technical climbs, culminating with the airy needle of the Grépon. Two years after that, he collaborated with the ace guides Georges Charlet and Alfred Couttet to make the first ascent of the massive north face of the Aiguille Verte, the hardest climb yet done in the Chamonix Alps. Brad was still only nineteen.

In 1925, the swashbuckling publisher George P. Putnam had launched a series that he called Boys' Books by Boys—nonfiction accounts by teenagers of their precocious adventures all over the globe. The first in the series, *David Goes Voyaging*, written by Putnam's own twelve-year-old son, chronicled the lad's participation in a William Beebe diving expedition in the Pacific.

It was the age of the Hardy Boys and Tom Swift, and Boys' Books by Boys captured the same blithe, almost cocky blend of wonderment and can-do savvy that infused those teenage novels. At $1.75 apiece, Putnam's series became an instant hit.

Today, the books, long out of print, are collector's items. One purveyor of rare mountaineering books, Michael Chessler, sells *Bradford on Mount Fairweather* for $200. It is thus high time— and a noble service to mountain literature—that the Appalachian Mountain Club make the three Washburn tomes available, with many of the original photographs, to a public too young to have known those halcyon days of teenage American adventure firsthand.

After Brad's first season in the Alps, he wrote an account of the Matterhorn climb for "Youth's Companion" magazine. Putnam came across it and immediately signed Brad up, even though, having turned sixteen, Brad was perhaps a bit long in tooth for the series. Recently Brad recalled the process of turning his 1927 summer's lark into a published book: "I wrote it in ten days in the Pensione Calcina in Venice, on the way back from Europe. Turned in the manuscript to Putnam, as agreed, on the fifteenth of September, with a batch of pictures. The book was on sale by November, pictures interleaved in the right places in the text. Can you imagine a publisher doing that today?"

Among the Alps with Bradford came out not only in English, but in a number of foreign editions, including Hungarian. The book sold so well, Brad was able to buy a Model A roadster with the royalties, and later, to help put himself through college during the onset of the Great Depression. A gratified George Putnam signed up Brad for two further books, *Bradford on Mount Washington* (1928) and *Bradford on Mount Fairweather* (1930). By the time the last was published, the author was twenty years old, and could hardly keep passing himself off as a boy.

It is beguiling to find on almost every page of these youthful works the very stamp of the character of the man who would go on to such successes in adult life: a buoyant enthusiasm for sheer hard work, a born tinkerer's genius for crafting gadgets and techniques to pull off feats that nobody had managed before, a quenchless curiosity about the geographical unknown, and a certain headstrong insistence on being the leader (in his whole climbing career, Brad never went on an expedition led by anyone but himself).

The sunniest of the three books is the Mount Washington volume, in which Brad transforms the misery of frozen gear and flattening arctic winds into jolly play. (One would give much to know what Putnam, whom Brad talked into joining him on one of his failed winter assaults, thought of this folly. In the photos, the publisher does not look happy.) *Among the Alps*, despite the story's culminating setback in the face of another violent storm on Mont Blanc, is also an unadulterated lark—one that offers insight into the risky and improvisatory nature of early 20th-century mountaineering. And the Mount Fairweather volume, which chronicles Brad's first expedition to Alaska, undertaken, precociously enough, in the summer after his freshman year of college, includes a cast of fellow trailblazers from the Harvard Mountaineering Club's formative days. One of the charms of precocity is the author's occasional striking of a valedictory tone, as when, observing a talus-strewn glacier snout, he observes, at the ripe old age of twenty, "Such a scene of desolation I've never before seen in all my life."

In truth, not reaching Fairweather's summit was, by Brad's high standards, an abject failure that would eat away at him until he made his first ascent of Mount Crillon, in 1934. There would follow a string of triumphs in the Great North unmatched by any other mountaineer: the winter traverse of the Saint Elias Range; the first ascents of Mounts Lucania, Marcus Baker, Sanford, Bertha, Hayes, and Dickey, as well as three climbs of Mount McKinley—the last of which, Brad's swan song, accomplished the first ascent of the West Buttress (today's *voie normale*) in 1951.

At twenty, too old to write boys' books any more, Brad turned to other horizons, still hungry for new challenges. In 1939, at the age of 29, he was offered the directorship of the moribund New England Museum of Natural History. Accepting the job, Brad became the youngest head of a major museum in America. Over the next four decades, he forged new territory as an aerial photographer, holding a fifty-pound Fairchild camera in his lap as, tied in to the fuselage of a bush plane with the door removed, he leaned into the wind to shoot his magnificent large-format photographs of Alaska's mountains. At the same time, he turned a dusty warehouse full of biological antiquities into the acclaimed Boston Museum of Science—an achievement he considers the crowning glory of his long career.

Among his other talents, Brad in his twenties had become a crack small-plane pilot himself. In January 1937, his longtime friend Putnam invited Brad to dinner at his home in New York. Putnam's beloved wife, Amelia Earhart, was secretly planning her round-the-world flight in a Lockheed Electra. The couple sought Brad's advice about the logistics of the plan. Implicit in the meeting was an invitation to Brad to go along as navigator.

Brad studied the charts, and without mincing words, fingered the critical weakness of Earhart's plan. On one of the last legs of the journey, Earhart would need to take off from New Guinea and land on tiny Howland Island in the mid-Pacific. With dead reckoning, that landing could amount to a needle-in-a-haystack proposition. But Brad saw the answer. Get a ship beforehand to stop at Howland and drop off a radio transmitter. With that beacon broadcasting a nonstop signal, the plane could home in on the island even in bad weather.

But the restless and congenitally impractical Earhart dismissed Brad's counsel. She chose Fred Noonan as navigator instead. On July 1, 1937, the pair took off from Lae, New Guinea, headed for Howland Island—and vanished into the decades of fathomless conjecture that have turned her disappearance into one of the romantic legends of the 20th century.

On that same day, Brad was high on 17,150-foot Mount Lucania in the Yukon. Eight days later, he and Bob Bates would make the first ascent of what was then the highest unclimbed mountain in North America.

Now 94, looking back on that pivotal choice between the flight and the climb, Brad relishes the ironies of fate. But not once in all these decades has he said, "I told her so." The moral of the story of risk is never so trite. As he wrote at seventeen, in the last line of *Among the Alps with Bradford*, "And, after all, there's nothing like the feeling of knowing that you've done your best, even though you've lost in the struggle!"

—David Roberts
Cambridge, Massachusetts
Summer 2004

PREFACE

I can still remember the conversation, the restaurant—even the table where I sat—when I first met with Brad Washburn. It was the winter of 1989 and I had been the Appalachian Mountain Club's executive director for only a month or two. Brad was treating me to a "welcoming lunch." Brad was a young, energetic 79 at the time, full of stories, experience, and advice. I immediately realized how much he had to offer to me and to the future of the Club. Now 94, Brad remains one of my favorite and most valuable teachers.

Not long after that first lunch with Brad, my wife and then young kids were with me at the snack bar on the summit of Mount Washington when a woman unknown to us approached, said "Andy, I know Brad will want to see you," and simply led us to the Observatory. Only after chatting with Brad did we understand this woman was Barbara Washburn, Brad's wife and constant companion who, in her own right, has made enormous contributions to the AMC and mountaineering through the years. Barbara has reappeared in our lives over and over. While on a trip to Alaska we encountered banners along the main street in Anchorage, celebrating the 50th anniversary of the ascent of Denali by a woman . . . guess who? Later, Barbara, rather than Brad, served as keynote speaker at one of the Club's annual meetings.

Together, Brad and Barbara spent much of the last century visiting famous peaks across the globe, many of which Brad photographed and was the first to map. Despite a life of unusual mountain adventures and broad accomplishments, however, Brad's favorite peak is back home in New Hampshire. The relatively small but unpredictable Mount Washington was Brad's first climb, the subject of his first book, and the site of one of his most complicated mapping projects. According to Brad, the mountain provides alpine adventure to rival the much higher peaks of the far-away Alps and the Alaskan Range—and he would know.

Though Brad's first book, *Trails and Peaks of the Presidential Range*, was competition for the Appalachian Mountain Club's

White Mountain Guide, early Club members were sufficiently impressed to invite him—then a teenager—to join. It was 1926, and membership was by invitation only. Three years later, Brad's "Sunrise from the Aiguille du Midi" (which he casually snapped while enjoying a backcountry breakfast in the Alps) won AMC's annual photo contest, and he was working on his fourth book (the third tome in this collection). However, these accomplishments made no hint of what was to come.

Indeed, over the next few decades, his pioneering feats and dearest projects would forever change the international worlds of mountaineering, cartography, photography, and science education. But Brad always returned to Mount Washington. In 1978, Brad embarked on a project to definitively map the Presidential Range. The Museum of Science and the Mount Washington Observatory sponsored the project. Ten years and 200 volunteers later, AMC published and distributed this map, which is still a bestseller today. All of Brad's contributions to the AMC community—including his submissions through the years to our journal *Appalachia*, annual meeting presentations and talks at chapter gatherings, assistance with fundraising campaigns, and the loan of his favorite large-format aerial photographs for exhibit at the AMC's Highland Center—have been generous.

We thank Brad and Barbara for their life-long friendship, and for their commitment to outdoor adventure and learning. Their lives' work can be characterized by projects that involved both fantastic adventure and scientific inquiry. Their very approach to life embodies the spirit of AMC's mission to promote outdoor recreation, land conservation, conservation research, and environmental education. We encourage our members and the public to experience and learn about the natural world first-hand because we believe that successful conservation depends on this experience. Proceeds from the sale of all AMC Books help fund our mission of protecting the outdoors, and we are happy to announce that upon Brad's request, proceeds from the sale of this book will specifically support trail maintenance and education in the Presidential Range.

AMC would also like to thank Brad's agent, Panopticon

Galleries of Waltham, Massachusetts, for helping to prepare the photographs for this publication. The photographs are a selection from those that appeared in the three original publications. We would also like to thank David Roberts for his careful reading of, and research about, the original publications, and for providing wonderful context for this reissue in the Foreword.

AMC is pleased to reissue *Among the Alps with Washburn* (© 1927), *Bradford on Mount Washington* (© 1928), and *Bradford on Mount Fairweather* (© 1930). It is our hope that they will delight readers and inspire them to seek adventure in their favorite mountain landscapes. For as these tales reveal, mountain adventure rewards both the body and the soul, and is best when shared among friends.

—Andrew J. Falender
Executive Director, AMC
Summer 2004

AMONG THE ALPS
WITH BRADFORD

BY

BRADFORD WASHBURN

WITH A FOREWORD BY HIS BROTHER

ILLUSTRATED WITH SKETCHES BY THE AUTHOR
AND PHOTOGRAPHS TAKEN BY THE AUTHOR,
HIS BROTHER, GEORGES TAIRRAZ OF CHAMONIX,
AND ALFRED COUTTET, THE SKI CHAMPION OF FRANCE

This book is dedicated to my guides
Alfred Couttet, Georges Charlet, and Antoine Ravanel,
without whom neither it nor I should exist.

CONTENTS

PHOTOGRAPHS

FOREWORD

For several years both summer and winter have found Brad climbing in the White Mountains of New Hampshire. In fact about a year ago he wrote a guide book to the Presidential Range. He has always been an enthusiastic climber, as some dozens of peaks in the White Mountains will bear witness. He has climbed one of them over twenty times. His big chance came last summer. We went abroad and spent two weeks at Chamonix, a great climbing center in the very heart of the French Alps.

After climbing a couple of small peaks he was seen by Father and Mother, watching through a telescope in the valley, as he reached the summit of Mont Blanc, the highest of the Alps. During the next week which was spent at Zermatt, Monte Rosa and the Matterhorn fell before his conquering boots.

This year Brad has devoted himself to the most difficult rock climbs among the Aiguilles of Chamonix. He has made several first and second ascents, and one peak may be named after him.

This summer my brother became a member of the Groupe de Haute Montagne of the French Alpine Club. This is one of the finest Alpine clubs that there is, because, unlike the regular French Alpine Club, one has to climb a certain number of the most difficult peaks before one can become a member. To the best of my belief there are only two members of the Groupe in America at present. The other is a woman.

You can hire a guide who will pull you up any difficult places there happen to be on a mountain, but Brad usually gets up by himself. He agrees with those who believe that mountain climbing is a test of sportsmanship, and feels that if he can't climb the difficult places without being pulled he really hasn't climbed the mountain.

People from every nation of the world flock to the Alps, both to see the mountains and to climb. The motley crowd that one meets in the huts is made up of the best spirit from every country.

—Sherwood L. Washburn
On board S.S. *Colombo*,
Grand Banks of Newfoundland
September 18, 1927

CHAPTER I

CHAMONIX-MONT-BLANC

It was on a late July afternoon of 1926 that I got my first view of the Alps. While I was standing on the flying field at Lyons in France I thought that I saw a number of billowing white clouds far off on the eastern horizon. But, as they never seemed to move or change a bit, I decided that they must be the peaks of the distant Alps.

Before long Father and I and another man got into a tiny aeroplane just big enough for three people and a pilot, and we began the most wonderful ride that I have ever taken. The machine taxied slowly across the field till we were well over into a far corner. Then it turned sharply, and the motor opened up to full speed with a roar.

We sped across the field like lightning, bumping very heavily at first, then more and more lightly, until, with a little leap, the plane left the ground and soared into the air. It was rather a scary start, especially as we missed the gable of the aerodrome's roof by about ten feet!

Once in the air we didn't go forward at all for nearly ten minutes, but merely circled slowly upwards to gain height. We were going to cross a range of mountains, and the pilot didn't want to have to circle for height in the bad air currents near them. When we were about five thousand feet above the aerodrome, we swung around towards the northeast and began to fly straight ahead at nearly a hundred miles an hour.

I could see people working in the fields like tiny, black flies way down below. Even the fields themselves took on a queer air. They all seemed to be so neatly arranged and fitted one to the other. The rivers, too, were different. They had a winding look that one does not ever see from the level.

A blue range of mountains now rose ahead of us with a river flowing at its feet. These were the Jura Mountains of which Caesar speaks so often. Now I could see very clearly why the pilot had circled so high before leaving Lyons. Even at the height at which we were we barely missed the top of the ridge as the plane passed over it. In fact we were so near that we could see the trees and foliage clearly.

The moment that we crossed that ridge the view began. As if by magic, the whole horizon, which had been hidden from view by the Juras, opened up into a sea of snowy peaks. And there, far off to the right, rose the glittering snow-capped peak of Mont Blanc, a whole head higher than everything else. It certainly was the highest peak in Europe and it looked it too. It was a regular old monarch looking down on all his tiny subjects with a very cold and icy air!

I was so held by the grandeur of the group of mountains right around Mont Blanc that I hardly had time to see anything else. There was Lake Geneva, lying peacefully like a great greenish-blue gem, nestled down among the hills directly below us. And far away in the distance the spires of some mighty snow peaks towered into the blue sky.

I scarcely had time to glance about me before the airplane ducked frightfully to the left and brought us down five thousand feet to the Geneva aerodrome in three great circling swoops. It was all over in such a hurry that I could hardly realize that we were in the valley once more and that no snow-covered Alps were in sight.

The airplane in which Mother and Sherry (that is what I call my brother) were in came down out of the sky in a couple of minutes.

The flight was over and the family together again. Neither of the airplanes had fallen and none of us were killed! We did learn later that the planes in which we had flown were owned and operated by a company which was supposed to be the worst in Europe. They were machines that had been used by the French government during the World War, and they were all ready to fall to bits!

We had to go through a short customs at the aerodrome because Geneva is in Switzerland and Lyons in France. However, none of our bags were disturbed at all and in a very few minutes we got into an auto which took us to the city of Geneva, about a mile away. There we had supper looking out over the lake, on the other side of which Mont Blanc was in plain sight.

Before supper, father had asked for a car to be ready at seven o'clock to take us in to Chamonix. When we were all through eating we stepped out onto the porch, and there it was. It was a big Cadillac; but I have never seen such a motorcar in all my life. It was no *ordinary* Cadillac. The hood over the engine was all nickel-plated, and the whole affair shone like the sun.

The baggage had all been strapped on behind, and we piled in. The chauffeur finished his work of shining up the hood and climbed in beside me. Then we started the second great experience of the day.

The town of Chamonix-Mont-Blanc is about sixty miles from Geneva by the auto road. And every one of those sixty miles is a beautiful one. Besides, we had struck the very best time of day to take the drive. It was just after seven in the evening when we set off, and in that way we had the evening lights and sunset almost all the way up the valleys leading to Chamonix.

The first part of the drive, although it was through beautiful country, was along the level, across a sort of plain. We soon went through the customs—this time going back into France again. In going to Geneva we had just crossed a little strip of Switzerland.

Before long the plain began to turn into a valley, and the fields on both sides of us got steeper and steeper. An hour out of Geneva still another change took place. The hills with fields on their sides grew much taller, and became mountains with great cliffs on their sides.

A roaring stream filled with water to the very banks swirled beside us part of the way—this was the Arve, a river which flows into the Rhone, and finds its source in the glaciers of the Mont Blanc range.

Still further on snow mountains appeared to the left. We were now going through towns that I thought I remembered having read about in books on Mont Blanc: St. Gervais, where a railway starts that runs eight thousand feet up the slopes of Mont Blanc; and Servoz, where the Arve races through a group of marvelous gorges.

Night was now falling. When we passed out of St. Gervais on the way to Servoz it was really quite dark, except for the moon which was rising over the mountains. The road began to have a truly alpine aspect. It looked like the pictures that you see in books. It was hewn out of the solid rock of a vertical cliff, the massive wall of rock rising up above us into the moonlight. Another sheer drop on the left led down into the valley, ever getting farther away below us.

We swung up to the right of the gorges, and passed Servoz with its dozens of tiny, sparkling lights far down in the darkness. Now we passed through a deep notch through the mountains. Then with a sharp swing to the left, we crossed over the Arve, on a bridge high over the gorge, and entered the valley of Chamonix.

I recognized it in a second from the pictures that I had seen, even though it was dark. There on the right, sparkling in the moonlight were the steep snowy slopes of the Aiguille du Goûter which run straight to the summit of Mont Blanc. That giant was hidden from view behind the Aiguille but we would be able to see it in a few minutes.

The moonlight was gorgeous beyond words. The fine spires of the rocky Aiguilles, or Needles, just to the left of Mont Blanc, would be lit up as clear as day every now and then. In a moment they would disappear into the blackness, as the moon ducked out of sight behind a cloud. Those pinnacles are the most wonderful rock climbs on the face of the earth.

The clouds themselves were quite a show playing hide-and-seek with the moon amongst those icy crags, ever whipped on at furious speed by a roaring gale of wind. It looked cold up there, frightfully cold!

The whole way from the beginning of the valley to Chamonix we had that wonderful sight. All was dark except for the little chalets (French mountain houses) perched along the slopes near the road. Once I even fancied that I saw a light (I really did) far up on the slopes of one of the large mountains. It was the little Chalet du Plan de l'Aiguille where we went before doing many of our climbs. I was destined to spend many nights under its roof during the summer.

Soon the lights of Chamonix sprang up before us, and in a moment we were in the crowded streets of the little village. It's almost entirely made up of hotels and shops, while the houses of the mountain guides and country people are grouped in tiny little villages that form a suburb, like a ring, all around the main town.

The driver skillfully piloted the car through the pleasure-seeking crowds, which always fill the streets in the evening, and brought us at last to the door of our little hotel—the Astoria.

Father paid him off after a friendly argument over the comparative values of Swiss and French money. You see, since the driver came from Geneva, he wanted to get paid in Swiss money. We were then in France, and Dad had already got all his Swiss money changed into French, so they had quite a time. At last it was all settled, and the great car rolled ponderously off towards Geneva. I went for my room at full speed. I was tired and wanted to go to bed, as the next day promised to be an exciting one.

I could see Mont Blanc very clearly from my window now, as there was no Aiguille du Goûter to bar the view. The night was so beautiful outside that I just couldn't get to bed, but at last I managed to wrench myself from the window, and sleep took me in hand in a hurry.

My dream had at last come true. I was in Chamonix—and there was Mont Blanc to prove it!

CHAPTER II

THE EARLY CLIMBERS

Between our hotel and the rushing little stream of the Arve, which flows through the very middle of Chamonix, is a little square. This is the spot on which stands the famous monument to Balmat and de Saussure, the two men who had most to do with the conquest of Mont Blanc.

The story of their many attempts, failures and final success is one of the most interesting of all those in Alpine history.

In 1700 the little settlement among the mountains, which is now called Chamonix, was made up of only a very few houses. Most of these belonged to the crystal-cutters who worked their trade far back among the mountains of the Mont Blanc range, in a place that is now called the "Col des Cristaux." To get to their crystals they went up the great river of ice known as the "Mer de Glace," then turning to the left they crossed another huge glacier, the Glacier de Talèfre, and on the Jardin de Talèfre, a little island of rock and dirt in the midst of these vast glaciers, they made their camp. Here they worked during the summer months, coming back to the valley every now and then to bring the crystals they had cut. In the winter their life was dreary. They had little to do but polish their crystals and at the crack of spring bring them to Geneva where they were sold.

In those days nobody was interested in climbing the mountains for anything at all but his daily work. The peaks about Chamonix were thought to be the homes of great giants who would kill anybody if he tried to penetrate them. Once a man made an attempt to climb one of the mountains, but an avalanche of rock killed him, while he was returning. For years after that time people were afraid of the mountains and left them entirely alone.

But in the vicinity of 1750 a young foreigner came to Geneva and heard from the crystal-cutters of the Mer de Glace. They told him that it was a frozen river, with waves of ice, and caverns so deep that their bottoms were invisible. The young man got so interested in the tales of these crystal-cutters, that he hired one of them to take him to Chamonix and show him the marvelous sight.

There was no road from Geneva to Chamonix in those days. And when the foreigner started out with the crystal men, the people of Geneva thought that he was crazy to take such a long and dangerous journey. The old trail followed the route of the road that is there nowadays, so it was no little walk all the way between the two places.

The young man, however, was well guided by the crystal-seekers, and they brought him safely to the Mer de Glace. He walked out onto the ice, but was so scared by the crevasses and caverns in it that he spent only a half hour there, and started back to Geneva the next day.

He was the first man to visit the mountains for his own pleasure. When he returned to Geneva, he stirred up the people there with his wildly exaggerated stories. And before long lots of them were making the journey to see the wonders of the Mer de Glace.

Above all the others, a young Genevan, called Horace Benedict de Saussure, was interested in this great icefield.

With a number of friends he visited it a few times, and then his interest began to reach still further. He explored the Glacier de Talèfre where the crystal-seekers worked. However, he was still not satisfied, and instead of turning to the left from the Mer de Glace, as you do to go to the Glacier de Talèfre, he turned to the right. By doing this he followed another rout of the crystal men, up the Glacier du Géant (the Giant's Glacier), the largest icefield in the Mont Blanc chain.

Before long de Saussure knew the ground about Chamonix far better than even the crystal-seekers. He was not only interested in the mountains themselves, but in their very formation. He was one of the greatest geologists of the century.

In 1760, de Saussure offered a large sum of money to anyone who could find a way for him by which Mont Blanc could be climbed. All the crystal-seekers gave up their work and went daily in attempts to climb the monarch of the Alps. And they were so eager to get there before their comrades, that they fairly stumbled over each other to be the first.

It was a long time, however, before any of these men succeeded in their work. One by one they gave up and returned to their crystal-cutting. They were evidently trying to climb the great peak from the wrong side. Naturally they were endeavoring to make the climb from the Glacier du Géant, because they had hunted crystals there, and knew the region well. But the great icy slopes and cliffs on this side of the mountain were too much for them, and finally they all gave up.

One man *did* stick to the job he had begun. This was Jacques Balmat, a young crystal-hunter, who had been born in Chamonix. He saw the mistake that his friends had made. *He* tried to climb the mountain directly up the slope that faces Chamonix.

The woods were very dense up the first part of the mountain, making the climbing tedious. But when he got above eight thousand feet (about five thousand feet above Chamonix), he found the going quite easy. The glaciers on this side were not so badly cut up by crevasses as those on the other side. Besides, they were not nearly so steep.

After three or four tries Balmat succeeded, *all alone*, in reaching the wide, smooth, and almost level snowfield which lies only a thousand feet below the summit of Mont Blanc. This expanse of snow is called the Grand Plateau.

Here he stayed for a few hours and studied the snowy walls which surrounded him on all but one side. He made up his mind that there were three ways to reach the top from the spot where he was. To this very day, the three ways which Balmat discovered are the only ones used for climbing that final pyramid of Mont Blanc from the Chamonix side.

The first way was by the passage now called the Corridor. To climb this, he must turn sharp to the left and gain the ridge which leads straight to the summit of Mont Blanc, by a steep ice slope. He then would have to follow the ridge to the summit.

The second route was to go straight ahead, and right up the face of the mountain. This way, because it lies to the left of a line of red-colored rocks sticking through the snow, is called the Rochers Rouges route.

The third way looked the easiest of the three. It is the one used most often today. To climb it, he could turn to the right and, by an easy snow slope, gain the ridge which connects Mont Blanc with the Dôme du Goûter. The Dôme is a great snowy shoulder just to the right of the final pyramid of Mont Blanc. He would then have to finish the climb by following the crest of this ridge, much the same way as for the Corridor.

The last way, besides being the easiest, looked the safest, because the first two were both made frightfully dangerous by huge pinnacles of ice, which often fell from above the Rochers Rouges.

Balmat was satisfied with what he had found. He was dead sure that he had, at last, discovered a way to reach the summit of Mont Blanc. He got safely back to Chamonix after having spent two days and nights on the mountain entirely alone. And he told no one of his discoveries but the village doctor, Michel-Gabriel Paccard.

The pair started out from Chamonix a couple of days later, on the seventh of August, 1786. Each left the town by himself, in order that no suspicion should be aroused. Besides the two men, the only people who knew of the enterprise were a few inhabitants of the neighboring priory, who were instructed to watch the summit the next day. In this way the two climbers would have some reliable witnesses.

All the first day Balmat and his companion climbed up the lower slopes of the mountain. Sometimes it was easier in the trees, and other times they found the climbing made more simple by following the edges of the great Glacier des Bossons. This glacier falls, in one unbroken field of ice, from the very summit of Mont Blanc to the valley.

The first night they bivouacked at the top of the Montagne de la Côte, the tongue of land up which they had climbed all day. You can still see there the big boulder, under which they spent the night. I saw it last summer, when I climbed Mont Blanc.

The next morning, they started at break of day, and climbed up the snowfields and glacier that lay between them and the Grand Plateau. At noon they disappeared over the rim of the plateau, and the telescopes that had been watching them from the valley, lost sight of the two climbers.

The two climbers, spurred on by the late hour and the nearness of their goal, took the shortest route from the Grand Plateau to the summit—that by the Rochers Rouges.

They found the snow remarkably hard and easy to climb over, and before many hours had passed, they were nearing the summit.

The news that two men were climbing Mont Blanc speedily spread about the village, so the priory was not to be the only witness of what was about to take place.

At twenty-three minutes after six in the evening the telescopes again picked up their prey. But now the men were visible to the naked eye. There they were! Two black dots could be seen silhouetted against the sunset sky—Balmat and Paccard! The whole village fell on their knees in silent tribute to the conquerors of Europe's highest peak.

At the same time that the village prayed, two voices might have been heard. Perched far up in the heavens, Paccard and Balmat knelt side by side on the summit of Mont Blanc to breathe a prayer of thanks for their success. Their voices, as de Saussure later said, broke, for the first time, a silence that had reigned over those masses of ice and snow since the beginning of the world! Mont Blanc was at last conquered!

De Saussure was at once notified of the ascent, and he came at full speed to Chamonix. He made several attempts at the mountain before a week had elapsed, but they were all failures due to bad weather. De Saussure had to wait till the next summer before he could complete the ascent of the mountain. Then he made it a purely scientific expedition, and took Balmat with him as a guide.

From that time on, Mont Blanc was climbed more and more often every year, Balmat alone reaching its summit more than ten times in his life. Towards the end of the last century climbing had turned into a sport.

Whymper and Mummery, perhaps the two most brilliant climbers that have ever lived, stirred up the interest in climbing the "Aiguilles" or "Needles" of rock which lie just to the north of Mont Blanc.

One after another, the peaks fell before the attack of Mummery, with his two Swiss guides, Burgener and Venetz. Towards the end of the century, when Emile Fontaine, the great French climber, came along, there was nothing left unclimbed but the slender pinnacles which adorn the slopes of the larger Aiguilles so beautifully.

Fontaine set to work (of course it was lots of *fun*) to climb these little pinnacles, most of them less than a hundred feet high. However, the actual height above the sea of most of these little peaks is over ten thousand feet, and some of them are much harder to climb than the big mountains on which they are situated.

Peak after peak gave in to Fontaine as they had in the older days to Mummery and Whymper. Finally, when the Great War was over, the only pinnacles left unclimbed were those which were so difficult and sharp that they had withstood the onset of all three, Whymper, Mummery, and Fontaine. A formidable little group!

After the war, what is called the "New School" of guides came into Chamonix. The young men who survived the war, wild with the desire for a rough, out-of-door life, and in wonderful physical condition, took the places of the climbers of Fontaine's day.

The guides whom I had last summer were both of this new group. They were the most sure-footed, agile, and strong pair that I have ever seen.

Snow-climbing is not so popular now as it used to be in the old days. The climbing of mountains entirely made of rock seems to be more generally liked. But, as for me, I can't draw a line of preference between the two types of climbing. They're both awfully interesting and I'm writing just about the same amount on each in these pages.

CHAPTER III

THE AERIAL RAILWAY AND PLAN DE L'AIGUILLE

When we were all settled at Chamonix, I began my climbing. The first few trips that I made were very interesting. On one of them we did three peaks that had never been climbed before, and on another we made a climb in search of rock-crystals. The crystal trip was by far the more interesting of the two, but the only trouble was that we weren't able to find many crystals, on account of the fresh fall of snow which covered the mountains.

Just before the crystal trip, however, I had made a climb among the Aiguilles called the traverse of the Aiguille des Grand Charmoz and the Grépon. The name (I guess!) doesn't mean much to you. But to the climber at Chamonix it is a different matter. The "Charmoz-Grépon Traverse," as it is called by the guides, is one of the best known and most difficult rock climbs in Europe.

Now, on the first climb up the Charmoz and Grépon I had gone with two guides, Alfred Couttet and Georges Charlet, just as on the crystal trip. The ascent was intended to be an expedition almost entirely for pictures. But that climb was a dismal failure. The weather was very poor and dark all the way to the top of the Grépon, and from there to Chamonix it rained!

Besides the weather, however, we had neglected one very

Georges, Bradford, Antoine.

important thing. As we were all attached to the same rope, we were too close to take pictures of each other.

We returned to Chamonix, a forlorn, bedraggled trio without more than four or five pictures at the most.

That very evening it was decided, in solemn family council, to launch another attack in the near future on the Charmoz and Grépon. The plan was made to take with us a young photographer from Chamonix named Georges Tairraz. Couttet could go with us no longer as he was engaged by another climber. So the party would be made up of Sherry, Tairraz, Georges Charlet, Antoine Ravanel (a guide to take Couttet's place, recommended by Georges), and myself.

The expedition was planned with great care, and we were to start at the very first sign of good weather. Tairraz's pack was all filled and made ready, so we wouldn't lose a moment when the time came. He had with him three cameras—a movie machine, with eight hundred feet of film; a camera to take 5×7-inch pictures, with enough film for thirty-six of these; and an Eastman panorama camera with enough film for twenty-four panoramas. Besides all this photographic stuff I had my little Graflex, and Sherry had a remarkably good little Eastman vest-pocket camera.

If we struck good weather, we should certainly do the Charmoz and Grépon up brown!

One time we thought we had found good weather, and all started out. But just as we were about to reach the beginning of the difficult part of the Charmoz, it began to rain. So we turned back in fierce discouragement, and sat in the valley to wait some more for good weather.

It rained steadily, and was cloudy for nearly four days. But on the morning of the fifth day, the sun came out, and just after lunch we decided that the time had come.

I rushed over to Tairraz to tell him to be ready at four o'clock. Then we telephoned the guides, and told them to be at the hotel at the same time. We hurriedly piled up our equipment, and got on our mountain clothes. By the time that Georges had arrived, with Antoine and Tairraz, we were all ready.

The provisions had been ordered, and were waiting in the hotel hall, and I went over to the bake-shop, down the street, where I got a couple of dozen rolls, to eat with our large supply of honey.

At four o'clock on the afternoon of August 9th the expedition got under way. We found an auto, which took us down the valley for a mile, to the foot of the aerial railway, which climbs the slope of the Aiguille du Midi for nearly five thousand feet.

This aerial railway is a great time-saver because it takes you up five thousand feet in only twenty minutes! There isn't much excitement in the ride, as the towers of the railway aren't very high, and the car you ride in goes pretty close to the ground. Still, you *do* go higher than the trees, and the views all the way are wonderful.

As you go past the towers that hold the wire up, there is a very queer sensation, as the car gives a little duck and jump. That is the only thrill of the aerial railway. The cars that you ride in are simply ridiculous. They look just like little bathtubs with roofs and windows. The seats in them are tilted, so that all the way up the steep part of the road, you can sit without slipping off!

When we got to the top of the railway, we went into the little hotel there (the Station des Glaciers), and got some fruit to eat the next day on the mountains. Then we set out along the path, over dirt and loose rocks, that leads to the Plan de l'Aiguille Hut, where we were going to spend the night.

Above Chamonix, to the left of Mont Blanc, rise the four great groups of the Aiguilles ("aiguille" is the French word for "needle"). The group on the extreme left is composed of the Aiguille des Grands Charmoz and the Aiguille de Grépon. Then there is a glacier called the Glacier des Nantillons. After the glacier comes the Blaitière group, then another glacier, then the Plan group, then the Glacier des Pèlerins, and finally the huge group of the Aiguille du Midi.

This great range of rocky pinnacles rises directly out of a sort of narrow, sloping plain of debris and loose rocks, gathered there by the three great glaciers which descend from the aiguilles.

Right square below the Plan group, and between the Glacier de Blaitière and the Glacier des Pèlerins, is a wonderful grassy slope, rising above the surrounding desolate fields of rocks. On this slope is situated the chalet, or hut, of the Plan de l'Aiguille. The Plan de l'Aiguille is the name given to this vast plateau of loose rock below the aiguilles.

To get to the hut from the top of the aerial railway we had to walk about fifty minutes partly along the level, and partly down hill over that plain of rocks.

About halfway between the railway and the hut we had to cross the Glacier des Pèlerins. However, the glacier was in very good condition (that is, there were practically no crevasses in it), and we got to the other side in less than twenty minutes, without any trouble at all.

The walk from the other side of the glacier to the hut was down a very beautiful grassy slope, from which we could look back, every now and then, and see the avalanches racing down the face of the Aiguille du Midi.

There is nothing more terrifying, even to *look* at, than an avalanche. We would hear a low roar behind us, and turning around, we could see that a great hunk of ice or snow had been melted off by the sun's heat, way up there on the snow ridges of the Aiguille du Midi. A little farther below, we could see that great block, now

A Study in Footwear Snapped on the Glacier des Pèlerins.

shattered into hundreds of tiny pieces, falling more and more rapidly every second. All the way down the face of the Aiguille, this
roaring mass of snow and ice gathered rocks with it, and came
tearing down over the cliffs, just like an enormous waterfall. Then
the noise slowly died away, and the echoes ceased, as the avalanche came to a stop on the upper slopes of the Glacier des
Pèlerins.

It always made me shiver to watch those terrible cascades of ice
and rock, as they raced relentlessly along. And I shivered all the
harder when I thought of how helpless I would be in the path of
one of them.

We walked briskly down the grassy slope, and in a few minutes
the sounds of the avalanches had faded away, and we were at the
Plan de l'Aiguille Hut.

I was much surprised to find that the hut was nothing at all like
the Couvercle Cabin, where we had stayed while hunting the
crystals. It was a real little stone house, with the outside covered
with cement, and it was painted white on the inside. There were
two rooms with plaster and wall-paper on the first floor—one was
a dining-room; the other a kitchen and guides' room combined.

On the second floor there were a number of nice little rooms, one of which Sherry and I took. It had *real spring beds* in it!

It was well on toward eight o'clock, when we had finished supper, and were up in the room watching the marvelous sunset out of the window.

There was a perfect sea of clouds below us to the west, and as the sun sank beyond the horizon, every single one was tinged to a brilliant red. It reminded me of the sunrise on Mont Blanc that we had seen on the crystal trip, a few days before.

It got dark very quickly, and the lights of Chamonix way below appeared one by one. Soon it looked as if there were a great luminous spider in the valley, from the way all the streets ran out from the central square, which was all ablaze with light.

At half-past eight o'clock we got ready a Roman candle and some red fire, with which to signal Mother in the valley. When the appointed time arrived, Sherry ran out onto the terrace of rocks below our window and touched off the red fire, while I fired off the Roman candle from the window.

A moment later we saw a light blinking furiously from the window of the hotel, far below us. We replied with a few flashes made by passing a hat before our candle.

Then the flashing in the valley ceased, and after having prepared our sacks for the next morning, we hit our beds with a will and dropped off to sleep in a hurry.

CHAPTER IV

THE GRANDS CHARMOZ

That night wasn't like the one that I had had on the board bunks at Couvercle! I slept, and I slept like a rock, until a man came to the door and announced to me in French that "my hour had come!"

You always have to thank these men who come to wake you, or they just go right on pounding the door down. So I thanked him heartily for his kindness, and then woke up Sherry. He had slept soundly right through all the racket!

As our packs were all made up, and our clothes ready, we were downstairs in just a few minutes. Then we went out to take a look at the weather.

It was crisp and cold, but not a single star was shining. The sky was all misty. Georges soon came out of the darkness with Antoine and Tairraz and after a glance at the conditions they declared it better to wait for a while to see what was going to happen. It was then two-thirty in the morning. Another guide had got up at one-thirty and said that then the sky had been all clear, so that didn't raise our hopes at all.

We all went to bed in despair, only to be wakened once more at three o'clock. The clouds were beginning to disappear. It was fine and cool, which was an excellent sign, and when we went outside, day was already beginning to break on top of Mont Blanc.

We had a speedy breakfast of honey, toast, and goat's milk (terrible stuff). Then, as Antoine and Georges weren't quite ready to start, Tairraz, Sherry, and I started on ahead, telling them to catch up to us.

The path swung in short zig-zags up the grassy slope, down which we had come the afternoon before. Then, when some distance above the hut, it bore off to the left in the direction of the Grépon. It now climbed the moraine of the Glacier de Blaitière, and began to cross the glacier itself. As you know, of course, a moraine is the long line of loose rocks and dirt at the very edge of the glacier, which the glacier pushes along with it as it moves.

Once on the glacier we advanced quite speedily, but Antoine and Georges soon caught up to us. There were no crevasses at all on the part of the glacier that we crossed, so we made just as good time as we had on the Glacier des Pèlerins the day before.

The way to walk, as we had found on the crystal trip, was to hit a slow pace and keep it continually, without stopping at all. If you stop often to rest, you get far more tired than you do if you keep up a moderate pace for the whole trip.

That of course only applies to walking on paths, glaciers or snow. Naturally when you have to climb on rock you must go very slowly, and stop often to make sure that the man ahead of you is in a good position, in case you should slip.

On the other side of the Glacier de Blaitière we made our way across a lot of moraine and broken rock. There were regular fields of it that we had to pass over. Then, by way of two wide snowfields that we traversed (as you know, to traverse is to walk across a thing without either climbing or descending), we finally gained the moraine of the Glacier des Nantillons, just forty minutes after leaving Plan de l'Aiguille.

There we found a big rock. Under this we dumped all of the extra stockings, and other stuff that we wouldn't need on the climb. When all was ready once more, we started off and left Georges behind the moraine to change to his climbing suit—a rather important operation that he had neglected to do at Plan de l'Aiguille.

This time we didn't cross the glacier. We began to climb straight *up* it. The first part was dreadfully slippery ice, to which my shoes even with their formidable array of nails would hardly stick. It was much easier walking after a few hundred yards even though the slope *did* get a lot steeper, because of the layer of hard snow which covered the ice. This had been deposited there by the numerous avalanches of the last week.

Our route up the Nantillons wound back and forth underneath a huge wall of ice, the edge of which constantly falls off, due to the movement of the glacier. The snow through which we were walking most of the time was gouged out into deep grooves by the avalanches made by these ice-falls.

These dangers of avalanches, however, don't begin until nearly noon. Then the sun has had plenty of time to melt and loosen up the great, menacing pinnacles of ice. (These pinnacles are called séracs.) As it was then only five in the morning, we were absolutely safe for a while, at any rate.

Nevertheless, time after time, people have been swept away by avalanches there, even at early hours in the morning. There *is* a certain element of luck in the game.

One story that the guides tell is about a young woman and a guide who went together to the top of the glacier, not to climb a peak, but just for the glacier walk. On the way down, they were running carelessly along over a part of the glacier where there are lots of crevasses.

The guide was going last, as is always the rule for glacier climb-ing. That is, it's the rule when descending so that if you slip into a crevasse, there is somebody strong above you to hold the rope. But this guide was a frisky fellow. Instead of the tourist falling in as is the usual case, the *guide* went through into a hidden crevasse! The young lady was running downwards so fast over the soft, slip-pery snow, which covered the ice, that when the rope jerked her, she managed to hold tight.

It was a terrific jerk, and she lost her ice-axe because she was taken too much off her guard. With that gone, she had nothing to which to fasten the rope, while she went for help, for of course she couldn't pull him out herself.

She sat on that glacier for many, many hours underneath the wall of séracs, which at any moment might have fallen and wiped them both off the face of the earth. But, somehow, all that day those tons of ice stayed fixed. Once in a while they would creak and groan, but they never fell.

The guide begged her to untie herself and leave him to die, but she stuck to it. Night began to come on, and she tried to change her position in order to get a little warmer. As she moved she found that there was no longer any pull on the rope, and moving cautiously forward, she peered down into the darkness of the crevasse. A low cry told her that the guide was still alive on the other end! The rope, during the day, on account of the sun's heat, had sunk a little into the ice on the rim of the crevasse. Now that evening had come, the water-soaked rope had frozen into the ice and was fixed there fast!

She told the guide of her discovery, and then, unroping herself, she recovered her ice-axe, and raced downwards over that treacherous glacier by moonlight to try to get aid up to her stricken guide before morning. She got down the glacier safely, and went to the Montenvers hotel, a favorite climber's resort on the way down to Chamonix.

There she got a group of guides who went to the glacier, and before day dawned they had hauled the limp, but living body of the guide to safety!

The rescue party was scarcely off the glacier before the wall of séracs, which had so long remained still, fell with a crash and obliterated the crevasse in which the guide had hung safely for over twenty hours!

That is the Glacier des Nantillons, and so it was when we climbed it. It is always treacherous—you never can tell what it's going to do. At six o'clock we reached the Rognon, a little island of rock in the midst of the glacier, where the French Alpine Club had erected a little refuge of rocks and galvanized iron.

We drank some water and tea in front of the refuge, and ate a few crackers; then we were off again.

Above the Rognon the glacier grew very steep, and we had to

cut steps in a few places, in order to be sure of our footing. We reached the base of the sérac wall in about ten minutes. There Georges warned me that we must climb very fast as we had got a rather late start and he wanted to diminish the chance of getting hit by falling ice!

We simply *rushed* upwards under the séracs, and over the great heaps of loose ice and snow, that had fallen from above the afternoon before. I heaved a sigh of relief as we reached a slope of smooth glacier, without crevasses or dangerous pinnacles of ice.

The slope of snow on which we then were leads to the foot of the Couloir Charmoz-Grépon. This couloir (ravine) is a long strip of very easy rock and snow climbing, that leads from the glacier to the ridge at the lowest point between the Grands Charmoz and the Grépon. It divides the two mountains, and makes the Charmoz and the Grépon two very separate ridges of rock.

We left our ice-axes in a sheltered spot on the glacier near the bottom of the couloir. Then we roped up and the climb began. To start, we followed the rocks on the left side of the couloir, in order to avoid the treacherous snow in the bottom part of it.

The lower part of the climb was extremely dull and easy, but, after a few hundred feet, we left the couloir on our right, and traversed for a good distance across the face of the Charmoz. By making this traverse, we got to the beginning of a large crack, in the otherwise absolutely smooth rock.

The crack wasn't either so steep or so difficult as those that were to follow, and neither of us had any difficulty in getting up it. We used the ordinary trick for crack climbing, of sticking your right knee in the hole. Then you advance slowly, but surely by jamming in your right elbow, and changing the position of your knee. Of course it's slow, terribly slow, until you get used to it, but after a little experience, you can shoot up a fissure like lightning!

Once at the top of this first fissure, we climbed fairly speedily upwards over very steep rocks with large handholds, until we reached the bottom of the second crack. There are three difficult places in the ascent of the Charmoz and this is the second.

However, it was the worst of the three bad places! It was an almost vertical crack formed between two great rocks. Its shape was much like a big "V." In the very bottom of the V was the crack, and the two arms represent the two big slabs of rock. The picture shows the place very clearly. The fissure was too small to jam your knee into, and too large and smooth to get a good grip in with your hand. It was, on the whole, very bothersome.

Georges went up it like a rocket, and then called for me to follow. My fix, I am afraid, was worse than his had been, for I had my Graflex in my little knapsack and it was nearly smashed to bits during the next few minutes (I thought so at the time)!

How I ever managed to get to the top of that awful thing I do not know. I jammed my toes into it, and pushed with my back (and the Graflex!) against one of the big slabs. Finally I got hold of a big rock at the top and writhed myself out onto a platform, where I stopped to rest from my exertions.

I guess that it was my sack that had made the crack seem so hard to me. For the first time that I climbed it, with Alfred Couttet as guide, I had no sack and found no difficulty there at all. I now began to have terrible visions of the next chimney, which was the last before the ridge. At its foot Georges took all the sacks and piled them in a heap. He said that they could be hauled up later, on a piece of thin rope that he had in his pocket.

This chimney is called the Cheminée de Glace (Ice-Chimney), for at all times the floor of the chimney is covered with a coating of thick, smooth ice. This ice remains in the crack because of the way that the rocks shield its bottom from the sun. No sunlight ever enters the Cheminée de Glace, except for a few minutes, just before sunset. For this reason, any rain that falls, or any snow that melts into the chimney fills it fuller with ice, and makes it very hard to climb.

The first time that I had done the chimney, I had had no great difficulty until the very end of it, where there was a great hunk of ice. This pinnacle of ice struck me full in the chest when I tried to lean forward. I couldn't, for the life of me, reach the handhold at the top, with which to pull myself out. I had struggled and struggled and *struggled*, but in the end Alfred had been forced to extricate me by pulling me out with the rope!

Georges and Bradford on the Third Peak of the Charmoz—
the Grépon in the Background.

On this trip, however, I was determined to do the whole climb without being pulled once, so I entered the lower part of the Cheminée de Glace in great anxiety!

To my surprise I discovered that the ice was almost all gone. Although it had rained a great deal in the last week, the water had been all fairly warm, and had actually melted the ice instead of forming heaps more!

The lower part had a rock jammed in it. This I had great trouble in passing, but I managed to get over it without being pulled. Once on top of the rock, I made my way swiftly up the easier part of the passage. It was just big enough for my body to squeeze through when standing up.

There were no handholds in it at all, and it was just like an extremely narrow corridor, tilted up very steeply, with ice on the floor. It was so narrow that if I had hunched up my shoulders I could glide up it easily, but if I straightened them out I stuck fast. Whenever I wanted a rest I simply straightened out my shoulders and stayed that way until I wanted to go on again. Then I loosened them up and put my hands way up ahead, pressing them for all I was worth against the walls of the crack.

That pressure was enough to keep me from slipping back, and by kicking my nailed boots well into the ice, I managed to squirm my shoulders to where my hands were. Then I put my hands forward once more, holding myself with my shoulders. That's the way to go up the Cheminée de Glace, and it's heaps of fun and work combined!

The ice pinnacle was now all melted away, so I had no difficulty at all in getting out at the top of the crack. From there to the ridge was only a matter of ten minutes' climbing like that in the couloir Charmoz-Grépon.

We were now ten thousand eight hundred feet high, and had only about a hundred more feet to climb before getting to the summit. But the summit was a good hundred yards away, because it was clear at the other end of the ridge on which we were standing. What we had to do now was to climb along the *very crest* of the ridge all the way to the top.

The sun was now well up and we could begin to take the moving pictures, or "cinéma" as the guides called it. We had had hardly any chance at all the take pictures up to the ridge, as that face of the mountain had been all in shadow.

After we had had a little food, the party split up into two sections—the photographers, and those to be photographed. The first was Tairraz with Antoine to help him. The second was composed of Georges (leading), me (in the middle of the rope), and Sherry.

The photographers stationed themselves on the last pinnacle of the ridge. Our group commenced the ascent of the next one, as soon as I had had time to change from my leather boots to a pair of crêpe-soled sneakers. Nailed boots are better than sneakers for climbing with tiny footholds, but for climbing where there are no footholds at all, and simply pressure or stickiness is needed, there is nothing to beat a crêpe-soled sneaker.

The "gendarme" or pinnacle that we were about to climb, overhung dreadfully on the side up which we had to go. Georges got in a good position a little below its base, and commenced to try and throw a rope over its top, with which to pull ourselves up. There was just enough wind to make the easy throw of about ten feet almost impossible. In fact, the last time that I had climbed the pinnacle with Alfred Couttet, we had taken fully fifteen minutes in just arranging the rope for that short place.

Georges at last managed to get one strand of the rope near the desired spot. The place was out of sight from where he was, so I stood on a small rock nearby and directed him, as he flicked the other strand over the right place. Then he took the two strands in his hand. Partially by pulling himself, and partially by walking up the face of the rock, he got over the bad place and reached the top to the little gendarme.

It looked rather difficult as we watched, but when it came to be my turn I found that there was nothing to it at all. The movie camera had taken the whole operation, and kept on buzzing as we made the ascents of the next three gendarmes. All three were small and very easy, the rock being full of handholds.

When we reached the top of the third pinnacle the movies stopped, and the photographers seemed to be working over still pictures of us. It was terribly cold with the early morning breeze, sitting waiting on the top of that dreadfully pointed rock. It was also an excellent test for dizziness! On our left a vertical wall of rock dropped a couple of hundred feet to a slope of glare ice. This slope in turn dropped some five thousand feet to the great glacier called the Mer de Glace, sparkling in the sunlight a mile below us.

On the right it wasn't nearly so bad. A rocky cliff dropped only about two thousand feet to the still dark and somber glacier des Nantillons. We were in a rather eerie position!

One of my legs was hanging over one side, the other was beating restlessly over the Mer de Glace. As a whole I was rather cold and uncomfortable, when we received word that the pictures were all done, and that we could go on again.

Here Sherry went first and Georges last. The guide always goes last in descending to take care of the ropes.

After Sherry was safely down, I took the rope between Georges and me, doubled it, and placed it over the very top of the gendarme as my brother had done. Then I took the two ends, the middle being firmly caught over the rock, and let myself slowly slip down the ten feet of smooth rock to the notch between that gendarme and the next one.

The next little peak on the ridge is known as the Carrée on account of its very square appearance from Plan de l'Aiguille.

It was all smooth rock on the side where we were, so we had to climb around to the opposite side before being able to get to its top. Here we let Georges go ahead again. It was not a difficult spot, but it was extremely *delicate*, so we secured his rope safely behind a little jutting-out rock, and paid it out to him slowly as he advanced. If he'd fallen then we would have been able to hold him very easily.

There were no handholds at all, and only very, very small footholds. He went forward cautiously and slowly, carefully adjusting his feet in the tiny roughnesses in the rock, on which he had to walk. Then, all of a sudden, he reached around on the other side of the rock out of our sight. And, with a quick movement, disappeared!

The corner around which he had gone looked so smooth that it seemed almost impossible to believe that he could have done it so quickly.

It was now my turn. Sherry fixed my rope in the way that we had secured Georges' and I planted my left foot in a tiny chink in the rock. Then I advanced my right foot very gingerly, leaning against the rock with my hands until I was in a firm position once more.

That was the delicate part. By reaching around the corner of the rock I *just* managed to get one hand into the hidden hold. I gripped it firmly and, with a little jump, swung through the air, holding on for dear life. I saw the glacier swim below me, nearly half a mile away, and then my feet landed on terra firma once more!

Sherry was soon with us. The next move was to get to the top of the Carrée. It took only about three seconds.

The peak was just too high for me to reach its top edge, while standing on a little pointed rock with one foot. Georges made it easy by standing on the rock, and then helping me up onto his shoulders. From there I could easily grasp the top and I pulled myself out onto it. Sherry didn't give Georges a "courte-échelle," that is, let Georges get on his shoulders. (Courte-échelle is the French for "short ladder.") So I helped Georges up the first few feet by pulling him. Then we two pulled Sherry up like a bag of meal!

We lay there on the perfectly smooth, flat rock basking in the sun, until the camera department of the expedition caught up to us. Then we descended—I first was let down much in the way that we had pulled Sherry up. Then Sherry came down onto my shoulders. Finally we both aided Georges to the bottom.

The Charmoz were almost over. The last bit of interest (the best) was the Baton Wicks. The Baton is a little finger of rock about twelve feet high sitting on the edge of a platform of flat rock next to the Carrée. The platform is so large and flat that it is called the Esplanade. It is about twenty feet long and ten feet wide.

The Esplanade was a snap to get to from the notch between it and the Carrée. I could just reach the edge after going up a little fissure. When we were all up there, I commenced the ascent of the Baton for the movies.

The Baton is so small on top that only one person can climb it at a time. So, in order to make safe the person climbing, you always have to throw a rope over the top, tie it to his waist, and always keep it tight as he climbs. For if you fell from the Baton you might even kill yourself.

It is a short but delicate little climb, much like the passing of the Carrée. I grabbed the edge of a big crack halfway up. Then, by a lot of twistings, I managed to get my feet where my hands were and slowly stood up in the crack. From there I could just reach a little handhold on the summit. And after more contortions I dragged myself out on top and stood up.

It was a *terrible* little spot! The top is less than two feet in diameter, and slopes awfully, so that it's hard enough to get up. But to stand up on that silly pinnacle with a drop of a *mile* on one side was too much to ask of anybody!

You can imagine the sensation that I got from standing there for *fifteen* minutes, while the others tried to get the movie camera going. The outer edge of the pinnacle wasn't on the Esplanade at all, and overhung slightly. So that when I stood up on top I could look right straight down for several hundred feet to the ice slope, and thence to the Mer de Glace, a mile below.

About two hundred feet away on the very summit of the Grands Charmoz we saw a number of climbers seated. They had just climbed to the top and had not done the "traverse" that we were perspiring over! A little to the right of the Grands Charmoz the massive Grépon towered up, cutting the blue sky like a sharp, black knife.

At last! They had got the camera fixed and the pictures were over. I hustled down and Sherry went up. In the meantime Antoine and Tairraz raced by us and got ahead before Sherry was down. They were going to get movies of us as we descended from the Esplanade.

Georges took out an extra rope a hundred and twenty feet long. This he doubled. Then he placed the middle of it over a sharp little pinnacle on the Baton, letting the two ends dangle

"En Rappel."

down the forty vertical feet between us and the next notch in the ridge.

Sherry, who was now down, was the first to go. He placed the rope between his legs, and then twisted it around his arm. Then he walked off the Esplanade backwards and kept right on walking down that vertical cliff till he got to the bottom! I followed him as soon as he was off the ropes at the bottom. The picture [on page 39] shows excellently how this "descente en rappel" is done. I think that it's the best fun in all mountain climbing, but it *is* pretty scary the first few times that you do it! It is called the *descente en rappel* because, in French the verb "rappeler" means "to pull back." When you are through with the doubled rope, and everybody is down, all you have to do is take hold of one end of it and pull until the whole rope is down. For, as you remember, the rope wasn't tied a bit, but just doubled over the little pinnacle.

Sometimes, when the pinnacle that you find is apt to *jam the rope* so that you can't pull it down, you place a little ring of rope over the pinnacle. Then you place the rappel rope through this ring, and it never sticks when you pull it. That's what we did three times later in the day on the Grépon. Of course you just leave the ring hanging there when you pull down the rope.

Georges pulled down the rappel and rolled it up again in his sack. Then we advanced once more—briskly now, because it was getting late in the morning, and we had to get movies of all the Grépon, too, before the day was over. Since both Sherry and I had climbed the highest peak of the Charmoz once before, we decided to pass below it, and not lose the time which was now precious for the Grépon.

It took us no time to descend past the summit of the Charmoz and thence, by a lot of steep rocks we got into the top of the Couloir Charmoz-Grépon—the lowest point between the two mountains.

CHAPTER V

THE NORTH PEAK

The moment that we crossed over the col and onto the Mer de Glace side, the wind ceased entirely and it grew nice and warm. The sun was boiling down in a very cheery manner, and we all sat down on a wide shelf of rock to wait for Antoine and Tairraz. They had been taking pictures, and had got a good way behind us while putting away the cameras.

Georges unroped us, as it was a good safe spot with a number of wide platforms on which we could sit as we ate.

The last time we had eaten had been on the Charmoz, and we were simply ravenous. We had stowed away a huge amount of honey and breakfast buns, when Antoine and Tairraz appeared. They seemed to be in the same state in which we were, and we all sat in a row with out legs dangling over that five thousand foot precipice, and ate to our heart's content.

We had some canned pineapples, and when they were finished I amused myself by throwing the can over the cliff, and listening to it as it dropped and dropped and dropped, banging and clatter-ing over the rocks for nearly a minute, before it was lost to sound and sight in the distance.

When we had finished, Tairraz and I walked along some of the platforms to a point where we could look up and see the top of the

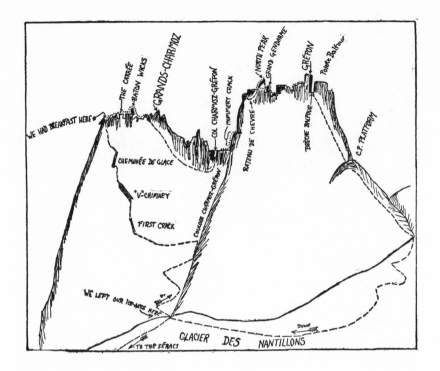

Grépon. A few hundred feet below the summit, on the Mer de Glace face I could see the terrible little Aiguille de Roc au Grépon, which a friend of mine from Boston had climbed for the first time a few days before. Its top had never before been touched by human foot. As for me, I do not see how any human foot ever got there at all!

As we turned about to go back to the packs and arrange our stuff for the climb, a puff of fog appeared below us near the Aiguille de Roc. In five minutes we were in a thick bank of clouds. I climbed up a little and looked over the Col Charmoz-Grépon. On the other side it was all sunlight! Not a single cloud was in sight. I yelled the news to the rest, and, much relieved, we roped ourselves up again and started off for one of the most difficult rock climbs in Europe.

Guido Rey, the great climber and writer, has described the ridge of the Grépon as "a series of remarkable coincidences!" As seen

The Mummery Crack. Bradford Getting Started from the Lower Platform.

from Chamonix, it appears to be far the easiest of the five Aiguilles, whereas it is the hardest. From Chamonix it looks like a long castle wall with turrets. From the Charmoz, the Grépon seems to be nothing but a giant knife!

Mummery, the famous Alpinist, whom I mentioned in the second chapter, was the first to reach the top of the Great Devil, what the Grépon was then called.

As you see it from the Charmoz, the Grépon is, as I said, like a knife. On its left side, and about halfway up, there is a big round hole known as the Trou du Canon (Cannon Hole). Mummery saw, from careful study, that if he could just get to that hole, the greater part of the difficulties would be over. The way that he reached it was by what is known as the Mummery Crack—without doubt the most famous single place on any mountain in the Alps.

The crack is a single rent which runs up the smooth and vertical wall leading from the Col Charmoz-Grépon to the Trou du Canon. Its height is almost exactly seventy feet, so when you have climbed it you have raised yourself about the height of a six-story house.

We climbed over easy rocks to a point about twenty feet above the Col Charmoz-Grépon. Here we turned sharp to the right and went through a tiny doorway in the rock, which placed us on a level with the middle of the crack. Here Georges, who was going ahead, told me to look after his rope and place it over a little nubble of rock, to secure him in case he should fall while climbing the crack. He then tied a piece of heavy twine about his waist, and descended very cautiously over the icy rocks to the bottom of the crack.

I had all I could do in looking after his rope and twine, and keeping them running out smoothly, so I hardly saw him climbing the crack at all. Once I heard him mutter something to himself and then he made a loud exclamation. His foot was jammed in the crack.

To get your foot caught in that crack is about the most dangerous thing imaginable for the first man up, because it is a very ticklish bit of work getting it out again without a fall. I watched to his rope extra carefully during the next few minutes. Luckily it wasn't badly stuck, and in a minute he was under way again.

Halfway up the fissure there is a little platform about a foot

Lunch.

square, upon which you can rest and get your breath. Once at the resting-spot, the difficulty is practically over. The lower part is climbed entirely by jamming your right elbow and knee into the fissure. There are no handholds at all below the platform! Above it there are a few little rocks stuck in the fissure that you can grab with your right hand.

When you have got in a standing position on these rocks, you can just reach another resting platform with a wonderful handhold for your left hand. From there to the top of the fissure is only a few feet with good handholds all the way.

Like all the guides, Georges only took about two minutes to get to the top. There he sat a moment to get his breath. Then he took the small cord that he had attached to his waist, we tied the knapsacks to it and he hauled them up one by one, laying them out beside him on the big platform at the top of the crack.

When this was done, my turn had come. Tairraz was stationed on a big platform to my right, ready to take movies of the climb. Antoine was right behind me to secure my rope in the way in which I had fixed Georges'.

With a heart beating like a pile-driver, I descended nearly to the bottom of the crack and crossed into it. I looked up a moment and saw Georges way at the top grinning down at me. He always laughed when I was in a bad fix, and I couldn't see anything at all that was funny about my situation! Then and there I made up my mind to comb that crack from top to bottom without being pulled one inch. Georges claimed I couldn't do it. I yelled to him to loosen up the rope entirely, and just to hold it so as to be a safeguard in case I should fall. Then I stuck my right elbow and knee in the crack. My left knee and elbow just slipped smoothly up and down, when I tried to find something to get a hold on!

It was just as I had found it the day that I had climbed it before. There was but one difference—this time I had on a pair of sneakers. That was a big difference however. Where the nail boots would slip, the sneakers stuck like glue. What was still more—I could not possibly get my sneakers jammed in a fissure the way Georges had caught his shoe. The sneakers were soft, and I could pull them out again easily.

In a minute I was on the first platform, puffing and blowing from my exertion. Twenty seconds saw me off again. There was a difficult spot for about two or three feet above the platform, then I got hold of a little stone jammed in the fissure. In a jiffy I had my knee on it, and with a little more twisting I was standing up.

I jammed my knee and elbow into the crack again and went a few feet more until my foot was on the highest of the three little rocks. There I rested a minute or so to get my breath, and looked down over what I had climbed.

I have never been dizzy once on a mountain, but I must confess that that one glance down the crack was the supreme test! The fissure went absolutely straight down for about fifty feet. The first platform already looked far away. And below the crack that awful slope of ice-covered rocks ran downwards, right to the Glacier des Nantillons! I turned to my climbing again with a desire to get out of that fissure as fast as I could. And I don't think that anybody could blame me for it! My left hand soon had the good hold, and up I went to the last platform, with my feet swinging wildly in the air.

Good handholds now appeared on the right. One more effort! I jammed myself into the crack, and with three great pushes and twists I reached the top, and stretched myself out among the knapsacks, panting for breath. That fissure is a great test of one's endurance, because every single moment all the way up, every one of your muscles and nerves from head to foot, is used to the very extreme. No wonder you are so exhausted when it's over!

Georges shouted down to Sherry that I had done the crack without being pulled, and challenged him to come on. Sherry started out, and a few minutes later his head appeared over the edge of the platform; he was puffing and blowing like me. He too had come all the way without being pulled. Antoine came next, and he was followed by a tremendous sack of photographic equipment. Before Tairraz had a chance to get to the top Georges, Sherry, and I were off again.

We went through the Cannon Hole, and then we climbed over some easy blocks of granite, until nearly to the crest of the first part of the Grépon ridge. A smooth wall of rock now confronted

The Rateau de Chèvre.

us. However, there was a tiny hole right through it. In fact, it was so small that Georges had to take off his sack to get inside.

There was a terrible little spot just before going through the hole, where I lingered for ages with a good handhold, my waist stuck between two rocks, and feet kicking in the air! I finally managed to get myself dislodged, and, by way of the hole, came out on the other side of the mountain.

I stood up now and surveyed the next difficulty. It is called the Rateau de Chèvre (Goat's Back). You climb it by placing one foot on each side of the rock, and then pulling yourself upward with your hands. The very backbone of the slab is a little rough, and by using your hands almost entirely, you can pull yourself all the way to the top.

When I came out of the hole, Georges was already halfway up the Rateau, and in a minute his feet went up into the air, as he got to the top and disappeared behind a big rock. Sherry was right on my heels, and to my surprise Antoine and Tairraz were already with us—they certainly must have hurried!

Georges cried out from above that it was my turn. But just at that moment the clouds rolled in. We waited for a couple of minutes until they disappeared once more. Then I took the opportunity to climb the Rateau as fast as I could for a movie. The sneakers stuck so well that I hardly had to use my hands at all, as is necessary if you have boots on. I got to the top in no time.

Sherry, who had put his sneakers on, now made just as good time as I had. When we three were all on top, however, I remembered that no still picture had been taken of either of us climbing the fissure. So I descended again all the way to the bottom, and had Tairraz take a couple of me as I climbed it once more. That's why in the picture you don't see the rope between Sherry and me coming down behind me. You can see *two* ropes leading upward from my waist—one is the end that goes to Georges, and the other goes to Sherry.

At the top there is an absolutely flat platform, even larger than the Esplanade of the Baton Wicks. On one end of it was a monolith, much in the same position as the Baton, but about three times as large. It was the north peak of the Grépon, only twelve feet lower than the real summit, which was just in sight, about a hundred yards away along the ridge.

The North Peak has been climbed by people many times, but they have always thrown a rope over the summit, with which to help themselves up. Last summer Georges climbed it alone, and without any rope thrown at all to aid him. If Sherry and I climbed it that way, we would make the first "tourist" ascent of the North Peak without thrown rope. Besides, it was a stunning place to take pictures.

When Tairraz arrived, Antoine gave him his camera out of the sack, and he went to the end of the flat rock to take pictures of us as we climbed.

When all was ready, Antoine leaned against the end of the North Peak and Georges got onto his shoulders. At first he swayed terribly. Then Antoine steadied himself and they got firmly fixed. Next Georges climbed up on Antoine's head and got hold of a very, very tiny crack running along the edges of the steep rock. In vain, he tried twice to get started and then descended to the platform once more.

He said that he would have to change to a pair of sneakers because his shoes slipped so badly. He soon had them on. This time things went well. Once he had his hands in the crack, he gave a graceful little leap from Antoine's shoulders and landed astride the narrow ridge.

The climb was so delicate that he had to keep moving constantly, for fear that he might lose his balance! There were no handholds or footholds at all on the ridge. The top of it was flat and about a foot wide, rising at an angle of about fifty degrees. He mounted this right to the top in about a minute, by walking in a bending position, and using the pressure of his hands on the sides of the ridge to steady himself!

Breathless, we waited at the bottom, and there wasn't a single sound to be heard, except for the clicking of the movie camera and our heavy, tense breathing. I gave a gasp of relief when he reached the top and took off his cap, waving it above his head triumphantly.

The North Peak. Georges is on top, Bradford on Sherry's shoulders.

I now mounted gingerly on Sherry's shoulders. Being taller than Georges, I reached the crack without having to jump. I struggled for a moment with every muscle in my body tense with effort, and with one hand I managed to get myself astride the ridge. From there to the top I did just what Georges had done. With my sneakers I had no trouble at all, and was soon seated on top beside Georges. Sherry followed me with success. Neither of us was pulled.

Coming down was worse than going up, because I could not see a single thing unless I looked between my feet. That was positively sickening for it made everything look upside down! It seemed as if I had been stepping for hours when I felt the crack in my left hand. I grabbed it, let my legs swing, and at last landed on Sherry's shoulders. He let me down again to the platform.

Even though we weren't pulled during the ascent of the North Peak, the very presence of the rope, and the feeling that I was safe with it around my waist, made me do easily things that would otherwise have been very difficult.

I don't see how Georges ever dared to climb that slab of rock without anything to give him the feeling of safety in case he should slip. For, even with the rope around his waist, he would have fallen a good twenty feet and landed on the rock platform where we were standing. The first man up must have real confidence in himself and iron nerve!

LE GRAND DIABLE—
THE GREAT DEVIL

The clouds were extremely well timed. Whenever we wanted to take a picture they would blow off. Whenever we were preparing our sacks or talking on the platforms, they stayed down tight so that we couldn't see more than twenty feet. Except for the difference in heat, being in a cloud is just like a Turkish bath. It's just a clammy, cold, disagreeable mist—a heavy fog.

Antoine and Tairraz were gone when we were ready to advance once more. Georges had had to put his shoes into his sack, and the two photographers had left us in order to have plenty of time in preparing their apparatus for the descent of the "Grand Gendarme" which we were about to do.

We passed to the right of the North Summit and, by slipping down a fifteen-foot crack just big enough to hold a person, we reached the notch before the Grand Gendarme. The summit of the gendarme could just be reached from the notch, and Sherry and I pulled ourselves out onto it.

It was a platform made of one big flat rock about four feet square, with a very small pyramid-shaped stone standing in one corner. While Sherry and I were lying out on our stomachs and enjoying the view, I heard a faint yell from behind. It was Georges. His sack was so big that he was stuck in the top of the crack!

He had no trouble in getting himself loose. And since the top of the crack was very near the top of the Grand Gendarme, he threw us the end of his twine and we pulled the sack over in the air. Then he slid the crack and was soon with us.

The Grand Gendarme is the largest pinnacle on the whole ridge of the Grépon and is made up of three, enormous, square blocks of granite. All three of them are as smooth as if they had been polished. Once you are at the bottom of it there is no way of return, unless you pull yourself up the rappel-rope! That is what Mummery did on the first ascent of the Grépon before the nowadays route of descent was known.

When we got to the top, of course, the photographers were already at the bottom and prepared to take us as we went down. They had placed a little ring of rope around the pyramid-shaped rock and had put the rappel-rope through that.

Sherry went off first, and slowly slid down the sharp ridge of the big rock until he was out of sight. We waited for a minute, and then his voice echoed up from below, saying that he was out of the rappel and that it was my turn. I took the two ends of the rappel-rope, one in each hand, and slid to a little platform about a yard below the summit. There I swung the ropes clear of the great rock so that I could slip smoothly. Then I took hold of the ropes once more and, lying on the ridge of the rock with one foot on each side, I slipped downwards until I was at the joining between the two upper blocks.

Here was a good hold for each foot, and I arranged myself into the ordinary rappel position, with the rope between my legs and over my arms, to descend the last two blocks of stone. At this spot the ridge of the mountain is very narrow, and as I walked slowly down with the rope between my legs, my body hid the bottom from me entirely. All that I could see was the great vertical wall of granite that I had just come down, clearly cut in the blue sky, with a drop of thousands of feet on each side. The reason why you cannot rappel straight down from the summit of the gendarme to the bottom is that all three rocks overhand a little toward the Mer de Glace. Why I had to follow the ridge to begin with was in order to get vertically above the ridge once more. If I had rappelled directly from the summit, I would have begun to swing freely in the air!

As soon as I was through with the rappel, I loosened the ropes for Georges and then advanced along a little shelf, where Sherry and the photographers were waiting. Georges hurried behind me and we were soon all on the platform, which turned out to be very flat and comfortable. Here he pulled down the rappel rope from the Grand Gendarme and put it in his sack.

The Vire à Bicyclettes (Bicycle Path!) was the next place to pass. We crossed over on to the Mer de Glace side. There, by taking a great handhold and making a little jump, we landed one after another on the most remarkable of the "coincidences"—a pathway, made of a single block of absolutely flat stone, between three and five feet wide, and nearly fifty feet long. On the right a vertical wall went above us for some twenty feet, and on the left there was a sheer drop of nearly a mile to the Mer de Glace.

We walked quickly along this, and mounted from its other end to a big platform at the very base of the highest summit of the Grépon. Here Georges mounted ahead once more (I had led on the Vire à Bicyclettes), and in a couple of minutes he was halfway from me to the top.

The climb from the platform to the summit we did in two parts. The first part is a fissure or crack in the rock almost exactly the same as the Rateau de Chèvre. That was easy. Then we walked along a shelf of rock for about fifteen feet to the bottom of the final stretch. From there to the summit was a distance of twenty feet.

The Final Crack, as it is called, rends the smooth summital block from top to bottom—a distance of nearly forty feet. By climbing the first little crack and using the shelf, we had avoided the lower twenty feet which are far the hardest.

Georges again advanced. Now it was extremely difficult for about ten feet. This difficulty was because the first part of the Final Crack overhung dreadfully. When Sherry and Georges were safely on top, I struggled and struggled to get above that overhanging part. The trouble was that there wasn't anything to begin with. I couldn't jam my leg into the crack and there wasn't anything to hold on to! Finally I got my sneaker caught on a little roughness in the lower part of the fissure. Then I jumped a little, caught a handhold way above me, and swung out into the air.

After fearful stretchings of my left leg, I just managed to get it back into the crack above the overhang. From there to the top was a snap, and for about twenty exciting seconds I raced up the last few feet, all nervous with a desire to get to the summit. I saw a little statue of the Virgin to my right and Georges was just ahead. Then I reached out, and with a good handhold pulled myself to the summit of the Grépon.

The summit is quite as large as the platform at the base of the North Peak. At one end of it there is a statue of the Virgin about four feet high. It is all made of aluminum and weighs upwards of one hundred and fifty pounds. Tairraz had helped five other guides and a priest when they brought the statue to the summit last spring. It was carried in three sections and then bolted together on top, where it is cemented to the rock.

I am not going much into the view we saw from that airy perch, except for saying that it was much like being in an aeroplane! The glaciers surrounded us on all sides, shining and glistening in the sunlight, which poured through holes in the clouds, as they raced by just above us. And Mont Blanc towered in a great mass of snow only a few miles away.

My sneakers were no longer of any use, as all that we had to do from now on was to descend. So I changed to my boots and put the sneakers away in my little knapsack. Then Georges, Antoine, Sherry, and I all posed for a picture beside the Virgin.

After Tairraz had taken the picture, Georges got a pineapple out of his sack and divided it equally between us. I threw mine away after one bite and watched it bounce down the cliff to the Glacier des Nantillons. Mother was watching us from the valley at that moment (through the telescope) and remarked when I returned that she had seen me throw something away! Imagine her being able, at a distance of about two miles, to follow our climb in such detail.

After Antoine had finished his pineapple he fixed the rappel-rope anew, in a ring that somebody had left over a rock on the summit. He descended and was out of sight in a second, swallowed up in an ocean of fog which was swirling up the Mer de Glace face of the mountain.

The summit, however, was free of clouds and we were in the bright sunlight. That is a trick which the wind often plays—one side of the mountain all black clouds, the summit and the other side in bright sun and clear weather!

Tairraz handed back my Graflex camera with which he had taken a picture of the group on top. He had also taken a picture of us all eating pineapples. But, to my horror I found that he had forgotten to change the film. Both the pictures had been taken on the same film and had been ruined!

There was *one* more picture in my camera and with a very nervous hand I prepared it for a picture of Georges, Sherry, and me beside the Virgin. Clouds were now swirling up on both sides like devouring, foamy waves. We would have to hurry, for the sun would soon be gone.

Tairraz grabbed the camera and we all sat down. Just as he snapped us, a rift in the clouds disclosed the snowfields of the Glacier du Géant in the distance and the sun came out. Then the mist closed in and the film was used up! What luck!

As usual Sherry disappeared right after Tairraz. Then I turned around and let myself off backwards into the mist. The clouds were so thick that I could barely see the tiny spot on which to stand a few feet below the summit. I waited there until Sherry had finished with the rappel-rope. Then I arranged myself on it, and began the descent of the crack known as the Cheminée Knubel, the most difficult spot on the whole Grépon—to climb *up*. Luckily, I was going down it!

I certainly can't see how anyone ever got up that fissure. The upper part was all right, but just below the top I simply swung out into the air, hanging on the rope, and descended that way for nearly ten feet. Then I landed on firm rock once more and slipped quickly to a flat platform where Sherry was. There was now no more rappel-rope, so I untwisted myself and called up to Georges that it was his turn.

At the platform I changed places on the rope with Sherry and

went first, since I had been there before and knew the way. By way
of a big crack in the ridge, called the Brèche Balfour (Balfour
Notch), we crossed onto the Nantillons side once more. We sat
there in the notch for nearly ten minutes, with a rousing good
wind blowing and clouds racing by, while Georges pulled down
the rappel-rope and slung it over his shoulder.

It was so cold and cloudy that we descended very fast from
there on, the going being rather easy over heaps of big rocks. We
only stopped once for a picture, when the clouds lifted for a
moment and the sun came out.

A little lower down, we placed another rappel and descended
in that way over some big flat rocks with no handholds in them.
That brought us to the edge of a little chasm on the other side of
which was a wide platform.

The only way to cross the hole is by means of a big rock that
fell from far above years ago, and jammed itself into the hole like
a bridge. You slide across this, lying on your stomach with a hand
and leg on each side, much like the first part of the Grand
Gendarme.

The platform is called the "Plate-forme du C. P.," because the
initials of two guides, Charlet and Payot, were found there carved
in the rock. They were the first two men to reach that spot.

I went first. There is a single little trick to get onto that big
bridge of stone. You have to reach around a corner with your right
hand and get hold of a rock that you cannot see. It's very scary to
do, but the moment that you've got the hold you're all right.

I remembered it from the time before, and arranged my feet so
that I could reach a long way without losing my balance. Once I
was arranged, I fell gently forward around the corner, and, reaching forward, landed on the handhold. Then I swung myself onto
the bridge and waited there to see to Sherry's rope. As he
advanced Tairraz snapped a picture of him catching the tricky
handhold.

At last Sherry was around, and we slipped one after another
across the bridge and pulled ourselves onto the platform. The
Grépon was almost over.

There we had a little late afternoon tea composed of no tea, no

"Passage du C. P."
Sherry Getting the Tricky Handhold, Bradford Sliding Across the Rock Bridge.

toast, a little bread, and some honey. Then we crossed the platform and after some hundred feet of easy broken-up rocks we
reached the Glacier des Nantillons once more. However, we were
now way up at the top of the glacier, and had a quarter-mile of
walking before getting our ice-axes at the foot of the Couloir
Charmoz-Grépon.

There the fun began. The surface of the glacier had been
melted soft during the earlier part of the day. But there was a layer
of glare ice about four inches below the surface. The snow on top
made the ice even more slippery than usual, because it wet it and
kept the nails on our boots from catching.

We must have gone at least thirty miles an hour as we slid
downwards, with a perfect sheet of snow shooting up after each of
us like the wake of a motor boat! In ten minutes we came down
the quarter mile to the Couloir Charmoz-Grépon. There we
stopped long enough to take up our ice-axes which we had left
there in the morning, and in a moment we were off once more.

In my opinion the hardest part of the whole day was racing
down past the dangerous walls of ice. Every pinnacle was just on

the verge of falling. The slope was not quite steep enough to slide down, so we had to run at top speed for a good two hundred yards, falling down and picking ourselves up, and twisting our ankles in little crevasses hidden under the snow. At last we were safely by the séracs, and, using our ice-axes as brakes, we slid down the final ice-slope to the Rognon.

There we had a good supper of chicken and jam and honey and bread. In fact, we ate *everything* that we had left there on the way up and were all hungry when we had finished.

The climb was now over except for the weary couple of hours of path which led through the semi-darkness to Montenvers, a mountain hotel on the way to Chamonix. We would have to spend the night there because it was six o'clock, and already far too late to go down to Chamonix by one of the little cog-wheel trains which run from Montenvers all day.

The expedition had been a success. We had taken eight hundred feet of moving pictures besides countless dozens of others. Everyone was satisfied and we all descended with light hearts.

But there is one thing to remember about that trip; one that always sticks in my mind. If you look at our pictures of the Grépon and don't find them as good as you think they should be, just think of the job it was to take them!

Half the time, a photographer is in more danger on the mountains than the climber himself, because he has to use both hands on the camera and yet stand firm in risky positions, perched midway between heaven and earth.

Besides all these difficulties the trouble of good light comes up. For ideal pictures on the Grépon you've got to have an early morning sun for the Mummery Crack, a late afternoon sun for the Rateau de Chèvre, midday for the North Summit, early afternoon on the Grand Gendarme, very early morning for the Vire à Bicyclettes, and finally mid-afternoon for the cracks which lead to the summit. Now, do you wonder it's a job to photograph the Grépon—in one day?

CHAPTER VII

A TRAGEDY ON THE HEIGHTS

Zermatt is a little village about sixty miles northeast of Chamonix, just on the border between Switzerland and Italy. Around Zermatt lie a group of the most majestic mountains in all Europe. The peaks about Chamonix and in the chain of Mont Blanc are terrific, but don't even compare in majestic grandeur to those heaped about Zermatt.

Chamonix is perhaps better for climbing, because the rock of which the mountains there are made is far stronger and less brittle than that in the vicinity of Zermatt. For that reason you feel a lot safer while climbing at Chamonix, and that's why I've been there twice and to Zermatt only once.

The town of Zermatt is still the way it looked many years ago. Only a tiny little cog-wheel railway comes up the Zermatt valley, and there is no auto road leading to the little town. In fact, there is not a single automobile in the whole town! It is an alpine village unspoiled by the average type of tourists, a difficult spot to find in Switzerland.

I made my visit to Zermatt in August of 1926 with one sole idea in my mind—to climb the Matterhorn—without doubt the most formidable-looking peak in all Europe.

It was a climb that I shall never forget as long as I live, for it brought back to me memories of the stories that I had read so many times about the mountain. About the Matterhorn and upon its tremendous crags have taken place more fatal accidents than on any other mountain in the Alps!

Although Zermatt stays much the same as of old, the mountains have changed. In July 1865, an Englishman, Edward Whymper by name, came there and in no less than three days he had conquered the so-called invincible Matterhorn with two guides, a porter and three English friends. But the Matterhorn was dissatisfied with being beaten. On the way down after making their successful climb, Whymper's party was overcome by one of the most horrible accidents that has ever taken place in all the Alps.

It was the Matterhorn's revenge!

My ascent of the Matterhorn was far from interesting from the climber's point of view; much less so from that of a reader! The mountain is but a series of big steps—a regular old staircase. And right below the top where it begins to get difficult, and where it would be interesting without help, the Alpine Clubs have gone and placed a lot of fixed ropes, which stay there all the year round for novices to pull themselves up on! It's not right. The Matterhorn should be left as are all the other mountains of the world, unhampered with fixed cords, for the climber to use his own skill. If he isn't skilled enough to climb the peak without pulling himself on a rope another man has climbed and fixed—why, he is not the man to try the Matterhorn. He doesn't deserve it.

That's not the type of climb that it's worth writing about or even telling about. This chapter is to be devoted to Edward Whymper's ascent of the Matterhorn—a feat of pure alpinism—a tale without which no book on the Alps is complete. It may be a terrible story, but it goes to show that the mountains are not always so gentle as they look. Sometimes the mountains seem to live. The Matterhorn was alive on July the fourteenth, 1865.

As you see it from Zermatt the Matterhorn is in the form of a very steep pyramid. You can see two great sides or faces, and a ridge which runs down between these faces towards the valley.

Before his final attempt on the Matterhorn in 1865, Whymper had studied the mountain from every possible angle, from a distance and from close up. In fact, he had already made seven unsuccessful attempts to reach its summit. He had discovered one very important fact during his studying. The ridge that runs from the summit towards Zermatt is not nearly so steep as it looks from the valley. The eye "foreshortens" that ridge and makes it look almost vertical, whereas it is inclined at only an angle of forty-five degrees!

Whymper arrived at Breuil, the little town at the foot of the Italian side of the Matterhorn on the seventh of July 1865. He found there that the two guides whom he had engaged for the trip up the Matterhorn that he proposed to make were both off with other climbers! That put his hopes to the winds. When he decided to cross over the mountains to Zermatt he found that there wasn't a single guide or porter in town who was willing to make the trip with him. They were all hard at work making cheese!

He went up and down the valley vainly searching for someone to aid him in transporting all his stuff over to Zermatt. One afternoon he met a young Englishman, Lord Francis Douglas by name, who was descending to Breuil. He had crossed over from Zermatt that very day and planned to go back on the morrow. As he had a guide and a porter he offered his services to Whymper. Whymper accepted the offer and the next day found the four of them in Zermatt together.

Douglas' guide turned out to be a great friend and guide of Whymper who came from Chamonix. By the time that they were all at Zermatt they were good friends, and had agreed to climb the Matterhorn together if they could find another guide and porter to go with them. At Zermatt they found another Englishman with a friend who were both desirous to climb the mountain. These two were the Rev. Charles Hudson and a Mr. Hadow. Hudson and Douglas as well as Whymper were all well-trained in climbing, but Mr. Hadow was not quite so skilled as the rest.

The day that Whymper had left Breuil he discovered that a party of seven Italians had left the village to attempt the Matterhorn from that side. That was now three days before, and if Whymper's caravan wished to be successful in making the *first* ascent of the mountain they would have to get going fast.

So the very next morning which was the thirteenth of July they all started out from Zermatt at five o'clock. Their party was composed of Peter Taugwalder and Michael Croz who were the guides. Taugwalder's two sons were porters, and the other members of the expedition were Lord Douglas, Hudson, Hadow and Whymper.

The day was a perfect gem. A balmy, cloudless one, not too hot but not cold. In fact it was just satisfactory. They climbed speedily upwards over the well-worn path to the little chapel at the plateau called the Schwarzsee, three thousand feet above Zermatt. Whymper had left all his equipment there while en route from Breuil to Zermatt, and they picked it all up, placing it on the backs of the Taugwalder boys.

Zermatt has an altitude of about five thousand feet. At noon the party had reached a height of about eleven thousand feet at the base of the great ridge of the Matterhorn up which they proposed to make the climb. This spot where they pitched their tent is the place where there is a little hotel now. It was there where I spent the night before climbing the mountain last summer.

Since it was still early in the day, Croz and one of the Taugwalder youths started up the face of the mountain in order to find a route of ascent. Thus they would save a great deal of time for the next day. The rest of them stayed near the tent during the afternoon and sketched the views or collected various specimens of rocks. Late in the day Croz returned with young Peter Taug-walder and announced that the mountain was a snap. They said that they could have climbed to the summit and returned before midnight!

That was great news and it was received hilariously by the crowd at the tent. That evening there was a beautiful sunset which promised well for the next day. And all the evening the crags of the Matterhorn echoed the songs of the guides and the laughter of the group as they chatted about the campfire. They had carried wood all the way up from the valley for the fire, since no trees grow any higher than seven or eight thousand feet up.

The next morning saw them off at the crack of dawn. They took young Peter Taugwalder as a porter and sent his brother to the valley with the tent and any other stuff that was no longer of use. The day dawned clear and cool and they made terrific speed as they climbed.

Whymper describes this route up the mountain as "a huge natural staircase." They continued the ascent at breakneck speed until ten o'clock. They always kept on the face of the peak and a little to the left of the ridge, at whose base they had spent the night, because the climbing was much easier than on the ridge itself, and because of the rotten rock on the crest. But on the face they found that it was more dangerous, for every now and then avalanches raced down it, so they were forced to keep nearly on the ridge all the way up to the shoulder. This is the spot where the fixed ropes now begin, and where they were forced to slow up and take caution.

The order of ascent was changed there on a snow-bank. Croz took the lead, Whymper came next, Mr. Hudson was third, then came Hadow, old Peter, and finally young Peter. When everybody was roped up and ready they started off. Croz then made the remark, "Now for something altogether different!" He was right. The rocks above the shoulder are very treacherous on account of their thick covering of smooth ice deposited there by the clouds.

The party moved slowly upwards, foot by foot, till nearly all the difficult part was over. Then they crossed a rather ticklish little patch of steep rocks which led to a snow-slope. That slope ran unbroken for two hundred feet to the top of the mountain. The Matterhorn was theirs! Croz and Whymper unroped and ran for all they were worth to the top. The race ended in a dead heat!

There were no tracks at all on the summit, and no signs whatsoever were visible to prove that the Italians had got there before them. In a few moments Whymper discovered them a thousand feet below crossing a little patch of snow. They yelled their heads off but could get no response. They *must* get them to hear or otherwise they would have no good witnesses of their ascent. Whymper rolled off some big stones and the others followed his example. At last the Italians heard—and saw, too!

They turned right around and began to run and did not stop until they were all the way to Breuil once more. There they told an exciting story of how the gods of the mountain had hurled stones off from the top of the Matterhorn upon them.

The summit of the Matterhorn is the best part of the whole

climb, for on account of the arrangement of the slopes and cliffs you cannot see a bit of the lower part of the mountain! I have shown this in my little sketch below. So when you look from the summit all that you see is a forty-degree snow-slope running off into the air, and then the valley far below. It's quite a queer sensation.

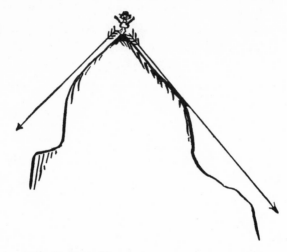

The Arrows Represent the Way Your Eyes Cannot See the Lower Ridges.

The successful mountaineers spent one eventful hour on the top and then started back again. They had placed one of the tent-poles with Croz's shirt tied to it as a signal of their conquest, in the very highest snow-bank of the peak. But as they had neglected to put their names in a bottle, Whymper stayed a little longer than the others to arrange a list for that purpose.

When all was finished Whymper and young Peter raced downwards catching up with the others just above the difficult part. Here Lord Douglas asked Whymper to rope up to old Peter in order to make them more secure in case of a fall. This was soon effected and they began the descent once more.

Croz went first, Hadow second, Hudson third, Lord Douglas fourth, then came old Peter, Whymper, and young Peter.

———

A few minutes later a sharp-eyed lad ran into the Monte Rosa hotel in Zermatt, saying that he had seen an avalanche fall from

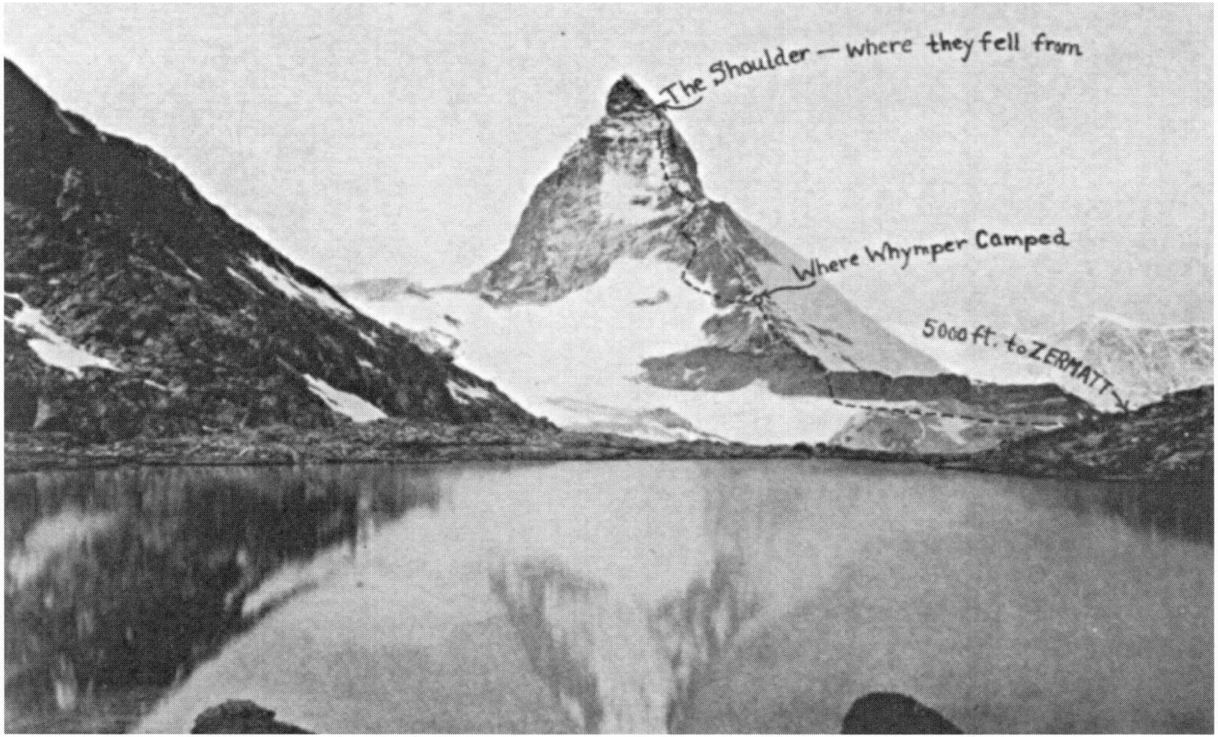
The Shoulder — where they fell from
Where Whymper Camped
5000 ft. to ZERMATT

The Matterhorn Showing the Route Up It.

the summit of the Matterhorn onto the Matterhorn-glacier. The boy was reproved for telling idle stories; he was right, however, and this was what he saw.

———

Croz came to a difficult spot shortly after Whymper had joined the rest of the party, and after he had cut some large steps he began aiding Mr. Hadow as he placed his feet in them. Whymper was hidden from the following scene so what happened will never be known accurately. But the first thing that he knew was that he saw Hadow's shoulders sway and go out of sight. At the same moment Croz gave a startled exclamation and he also disappeared. Then Hudson and Douglas were dragged from their feet by the jerking of the rope.

Taugwalder, Whymper, and young Peter held firm. It was the supreme test. Could they hold the four men? Yes, but—there was a sharp snap, the rope parted between Douglas and old Peter Taugwalder. The four men, lying on their backs, raced headlong down the slope of ice and rocks and disappeared, one by one, over the cliff of four thousand feet which drops to the Matterhorn glacier. They were lost!

For a half-hour all that the Taugwalders could do was to weep and moan. They had lost all their senses so great was their grief. They would neither go up nor down. They wailed incessantly, "We are lost, we are lost!" Whymper could do nothing with them for nearly an hour. Then they descended, shaking in every limb, and, as Whymper describes, old Peter would turn about every now and then and would mutter with an ashen face, "I cannot, I cannot." Heaven only knows how that brave Englishman ever guided his guides to the base of that mighty peak. But he did it, and at six in the evening, three hours after the accident, they reached the site of their tent. There they gathered the few things that they and their lost companions had owned into a bundle and started for Zermatt.

The difficulties were over, but not the excitement or the horror. None but the words of Whymper himself can describe the next few moments.

"At about six P.M. we arrived at the snow upon the ridge descending towards Zermatt, and all peril was over. We frequently looked, but in vain, for traces of our unfortunate comrades; we bent over the ridge and cried to them, but no sound returned. Convinced at last that they were neither within sight nor hearing we ceased from our useless efforts; and, too cast down for speech, silently gathered up our things and the little effects of those that were lost, preparatory to continuing the descent. When, Lo! a mighty arch appeared, rising above the Lyskamm (a neighboring peak), high into the sky. Pale, colorless, and noiseless, but perfectly sharp and defined, except where it was lost in the clouds, this unearthly apparition seemed like a vision from another world; and, almost appalled, we watched with amazement the gradual development of two vast crosses, one on either side. If the Taugwalders had not been the first to perceive it, I should have doubted my senses. They thought it had some connection with the accident, and I, after a while, that it might bear some relation to ourselves. But our movements had no effect upon it. The spectral forms remained motionless. It was a fearful and wonderful sight; unique in my experience, and impressive beyond description, coming at such a moment."

The Taugwalders lay with their faces covered until this horrible vision had vanished. It was like a summons to them from the world beyond. It seemed as though the Heavens had been opened to them by their dead companions, who beckoned for them to follow.

It finally faded away into the evening and the darkness. Then only did they uncover their eyes and descend on the run, after the never-tiring Whymper. They were forced to spend the night a little above Zermatt in the woods under a sheltering rock. Early in the morning they were off once more and reached Zermatt a few hours later.

They walked silently through the streets to the Monte Rosa hotel. There they stopped. The proprietor, a Mr. Seiler, came out to meet them and give them congratulations on their success. He looked Whymper in the face, then his look of joy faded out. "The Taugwalders and I have returned," was the reply to the silent question. Seiler burst into tears. The Matterhorn was conquered but it had cost dearly. The spirits of the mountain had taken their toll!

CHAPTER VIII

THE LOWER SLOPES
OF MONT BLANC

All summer Sherry and I postponed the ascent of Mont Blanc, because we wanted to be in the very best of physical condition when we did it. I also wanted to get pictures of the ascent for this book. These I had been unable to get last year when I climbed it, on account of the severe cold which we encountered on the last ridge.

The climb in itself is really not a very difficult one. Of course, it is not at all like the Grépon or any of the rock climbs. As a matter of fact, you do not lay your foot on a bit of rock all the way up the last half of Mont Blanc, except for the little heap of stones at the Grands Mulets where you spend the night.

It's all snow; just oceans and oceans of it, billowing upwards in extremely steep slopes. The lower slopes are full of crevasses, while the upper ones which run right to the summit are always smooth. The crevasses in the upper slopes, if ever they do form, are instantly filled up with the new snow which falls there constantly all the year round.

Mont Blanc was postponed so many times that we finally saw that we might not be able to climb it at all! The weather got continually worse and worse. We all sat in the valley and ate ice cream and had afternoon tea. We couldn't do any climbing at all.

So much snow fell during the rainstorms we had in the valley that the Grépon (when it appeared for a few moments one day) looked like a snow-peak. It was just plastered with sticky white snow from top to bottom, and so were all the rest of the Aiguilles. Georges said that, except for the lack of snow in the valley, it as just like winter.

After this continual bad weather had been going for over a week, a bright idea struck Georges and me while in consultation. Mont Blanc would be utterly impossible on foot for the next week, even if we were to have four successive days of good weather, on account of the tremendous amount of new snow that had fallen. Why not try the climb *on skis?* That would certainly be a grand novelty in the early part of August. And to have a ski trip in the middle of summer would be positively thrilling.

Of course I didn't have any skis, and neither did Sherry. But Sherry claimed that he hadn't skied enough to try such a difficult trip, and that he would plan to do it on snow-shoes.

Our plans were made very swiftly. Georges and I went over to a regular factory where they made skis and sleds. There we got two wonderful light pairs of skis—one for me, and another to bring back to a friend in America. At the same time, Sherry went off with Antoine to another store and got a pair of French snow-shoes. They were the funniest looking snow-shoes that I have ever seen. Instead of being made of gut or rawhide they were strung with twine. Nevertheless, they were the only things that he could get and they would have to do.

It was raining hard when we got the snow-shoes, but, like magic, the next day dawned clear as crystal. Every cloud had cleared away and a north wind was blowing. That is a sure sign of good weather at Chamonix. But with a north wind it is always cold. You can't very often get a good clear day that is warm.

We got up good and early and telephoned Georges and Antoine to come down as soon as they could, with all the stuff they needed for Mont Blanc. I went out and bought an extra muffler and some special, rubber-lined, windproof gloves for skiing. Then I got some mittens to put inside the rubber gloves and returned to the hotel to get my mountain clothes on.

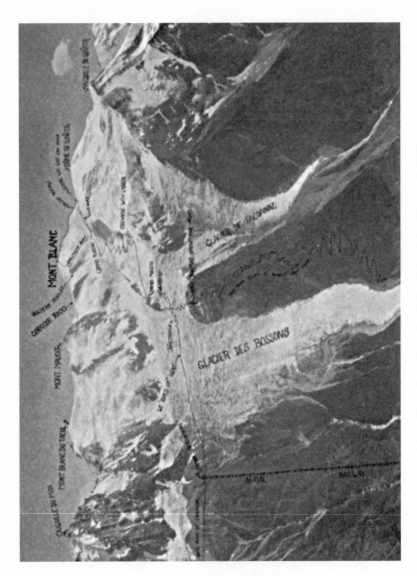

Mont Blanc Seen from the Other Side of the Chamonix Valley.

I had got my boots all greased and on when the guides arrived. We ordered provisions for two days from the hotel—chicken and honey, bread, sardines, cold meats, and chocolate. Then, when it was all packed into the sacks, we said goodbye to everyone and set off.

I have marked out on the picture just the routes that I've followed up Mont Blanc the two times that I have been on it. Last year I had to walk for eight hours, all the way from the valley to the Grands Mulets, where you spend the night. This year we took the aerial railway, which had just been completed, and walked only an hour and three-quarters across the Glacier des Bossons to the same place!

What's more, the aerial railway saves a lot of your strength, and on Mont Blanc strength and endurance are what you need. You don't need to have any skill to get to the top of that heap of ice and snow! That's why we waited so long before doing it—so that we would be just as strong as possible and in the very best of condition for the climb.

We made quite a hit, going through the center of Chamonix with skis on our shoulders, as the August sun baked down! But all the guides admitted that that was the only way to get to the top of Mont Blanc. The soft, new snow, they said, was at least two feet deep. To climb the mountain without skis or snowshoes we'd have had to wade along through the snow deeper than our knees.

The same aerial railway that had taken us up the day before we had climbed the Grépon, again lifted us from the valley to a height of over eight thousand feet. That is vertically a little over a mile above Chamonix and it took only twenty-five minutes.

When we reached the Station des Glaciers at the top of the line, we shouldered our skis and began to cross the Glacier des Bossons towards the Grands Mulets. The little hut called the Grands Mulets is placed on a tiny island of rock, square in the middle of the icy sea of the Glacier des Bossons. It is ten thousand feet high, and thus it leaves about five and a half thousand feet of climbing for the second day.

The Glacier des Bossons is exceptionally interesting. It isn't

like the Mer de Glace with its smooth waves almost free of great
séracs and crevasses. The Bossons provides a lot of excitement in
the way of crossing crevasses, and even in actually climbing the
séracs or pinnacles of ice.

As you can see in the picture, a great tongue of land runs way
up the side of Mont Blanc between the glaciers of Taconnaz and
Bossons. That, by the way, is the route that I followed to the
Grands Mulets last year. The old trail leads from the valley the
whole way up the tongue and then by the glacier to the hut.

This tongue is the cause for most of the crevasses just below the
Grands Mulets. The glacier comes down the mountain slowly but
surely in a wide sheet of ice, until it reaches the Grands Mulets
Rocks. There it is split in two. Then it joins again, just below the
islet, and flows like a vast sea to the top of the tongue of land
which is called the Montagne de la Côte. There again it is split in
two. This time the two parts continue separately, one being the
Glacier des Bossons and the other the Glacier de Taconnaz. That
wide field of ice between the Grands Mulets and the Montagne de
la Côte is called the Jonction, because it is the junction of two
great glaciers, and also the icefield which has been split in two by
the Grands Mulets Rocks.

This splitting-up makes the ice get all mixed up, and piled around
into huge heaps which at some seasons are almost unpassable. Those
of you who have read *David Goes to Greenland* must know what
"pack ice" is. The Jonction is like a large field of that pack ice.

Last year when I climbed Mont Blanc it had been a very cold
summer, and the crevasses of the Jonction were nearly all filled in
with snow. But this year you should have seen them! You couldn't
see one way or the other the ice was piled up so high.

We didn't use rope for the first part of the glacier, but when we
reached the Jonction we put it on for safety.

This year we had the same porter that I had last year for the
ascent of Mont Blanc. His name was Georges Cachat. It's always
necessary to have a porter on that climb because it's so long and
fatiguing for anyone under twenty-five years old, that it is good to
go without anything on your back at all.

As I was saying, we put on the rope and began to cross the Jonction. Georges, Cachat, and I were on one rope. That one went first, and I was tied in the middle. Sherry and Antoine were on another, and went behind us to take photographs.

We crossed crevasse after crevasse, always using the same method for safety, although the guides were somewhat bothered by their load of skis. I stood still and held Georges' rope as he tested the snow with his ice-axe and then advanced to the other side across the snow bridge. Then, when he was safely fixed, both he and Cachat saw to my rope as I crossed. Finally I took care of Cachat's as he crossed.

That is about the safest way (it *is* the safest way) to cross a crevasse, and that's the way that we always did it. Because if anyone slips while going over there is always somebody with a good footing to help him get out of the hole.

The snow bridges were really terribly scary. In some places I actually had to sit down astride them, because they were too narrow for my feet and, usually, too weak to walk on. Once seated firmly, I pushed myself forward with my hands, letting each leg dangle into the crevasse on one side of the narrow bridge.

Some of these holes dropped away through the darkness for more than a hundred feet into the depths of the glacier. Others were only a few feet deep. The ice in these cracks was a wonderful, light bluish-green color near the surface. This melted darker and darker as the crevasses got deeper, till it faded away entirely to the inky blackness which led to the bottom. There were lots of crevasses whose bottoms were so far down that the darkness made them impossible to see!

Last year in that very spot I saw a German climber fall into one of those awful holes. He tried to cross a snow bridge too fast and it broke in two where he stepped on it. Down he went into the crevasse, yelling wildly and grabbing at the slippery ice with his hands! Luckily the crevasse was only about ten feet deep. That is, the place where he landed was that deep, but about two feet from the little platform where he stopped the hole dropped away for nearly forty feet! In an instant the two other men on his rope caught him up tight. Then they lowered him to the little platform and let him rest from the shock there. When he was all right once more, my guide and porter, together with his guides pulled him out like a bag of meal! When they did it I got onto a nearby slab of ice and got two wonderful pictures of them dragging the poor fellow out.

A little bit above the Jonction there were two enormous crevasses which were so wide that we couldn't have ever got across them without the ladders that we found there. The men who carry the provisions from the Station des Glaciers to the Grands Mulets put them there so as to make it easier for them with their heavy packs.

Above the second ladder we took off the rope. From there a short walk up over a wonderful, smooth snowfield brought us to the Grands Mulets. One hour and forty minutes' easy walk (except for the Jonction!) this year, compared with the seven and one-half grueling hours that I had last summer! I blessed the man who had put up the aerial railway.

The first place to which I went when we arrived at the cabin was the little room where I spent the night last year. There, on the wall behind the bed, was the following inscription in neat penciled letters:

> H. B. Washburn, Jr.,
> August 6, 1926—Climbed Mont Blanc
> from Chamonix.

If "fools' names always appear in public places" everybody that ever went to the Grands Mulets is a fool! The wall is simply black with names that climbers have penciled on, just as they go to bed the night before making the climb.

We had a still better supper than the one that I had there last year, because of the fact, I suppose, that the men who lug up the food have to walk so much shorter a distance on account of the aerial road. That aerial road has simplified the packers' work from four miles steep uphill walking, to a walk of one mile on the level and a half-mile uphill! It has made some difference to those men, all right.

I toasted some of our buns on the stove and then ate them with the honey that Cachat had lugged up for us. I lived on this instead of the cast-iron steak that Sherry and a couple of other mountaineers seemed to eat with relish. I can't see how anyone can chew for fifteen minutes on an old dried-up piece of beef, half the size of a pencil, and then claim to have got more nourishment out of it than a good combination of butter, honey, and toast! I can't understand.

CHAPTER IX

SKIING ABOUT
THE ROOF OF EUROPE

I think that that night at the Grands Mulets was the coldest that I have ever had. I had to keep on all my clothes, together with a special, fur-lined Eskimo hood in order to be *half* warm enough to sleep.

The wind howled and whistled about that little hut, and way down deep in my mind I was absolutely sure that we wouldn't get to the top of Mont Blanc the next day. When I'd climbed before there hadn't been any wind at all at the hut, and even then, on the final ridge, we'd found a good little breeze blowing. It had been so cold that Cachat had frozen his hand!

What would it be up there with this wind? Besides, last year it was warm when we started from the cabin.

In the midst of one of my many naps I was awakened. The hour had come. It was quarter of two in the morning and was time to get up. As I didn't have any clothes *off*, it didn't take me a very long time to dress. Sherry, for the same reason, was equally speedy, and we went to the kitchen together. There we prepared our breakfast of toast, honey, and malted milk. That was the first time I had ever drunk malted milk on a mountain, and it certainly was the best tasting drink that I had ever had for a mountain breakfast.

You know that you must be very careful what you eat when you

The Author at the Grands Mulets.

climb, as you are using your body to the very last bit, and it always must have the right kind of fuel to keep it going. Before this summer, I never have been able to find anything to drink that would taste right at breakfast, eaten just after midnight. But, after that one drink of malted milk I have never drunk anything else!

Our breakfast was soon finished and we made our way into the guides' room to see how they were coming on. One flickering candle was the only thing that lighted up their large room. They were almost ready, too. I got some of my camera supplies from Georges and asked his opinion on the weather. He said that it was too warm to be a good day!

When I protested, he took me outside. Sure enough, he was right. The wind that had been so cold all night, had swung around into the south and was now very warm. Besides, the moon had a big white ring around it. Nevertheless, he said that we had best go as far as the Grand Plateau and see there what the weather would be. You remember, of course, from the second chapter where the Grand Plateau is—right below the summit of Mont Blanc. It is the halfway mark from the Grands Mulets to the top, even though it is nearly two-thirds of the way up in altitude. This is because, above the plateau, the route you follow is so crooked it makes it lots longer.

We were all ready by two-thirty, and taking our skis, we descended the little heap of rocks before the hut, to the edge of the glacier and the snowfields.

The guides had skied up for nearly a mile, during our supper, the evening before. They had worn a wonderful path in the snow, and we followed this, not yet bothering to put on our skis, because the walking was so much quicker without them. Sherry, however, did put on his snow-shoes, for they were small and light, and it didn't make much difference to him whether they were off or on. We carried the skis strapped together on our right shoulders.

The silence was so deep that I could almost hear it. The only noise that I could make out was the steady crunch, crunch, crunch of Georges' shoes in the snow, and the occasional rumble of the glacier as it slowly moved downwards. A glacier's rumble is much like the roar of distant thunder, and is very spooky as it echoes and re-echoes among the mountains.

The wind had all gone down, and, as we trudged upward, it grew warmer every minute. It was either a sure sign of stormy weather or of heavy winds after sunrise.

Two Germans and their guides, who were climbing right behind us, turned and went back to the Grand Mulets. They said that they had had enough of the old mountain already, and knew that they couldn't get to the top if they kept on. But we all agreed to push ahead and take the chances on the weather, so as not to lose a good day if it should turn out that way.

Forty minutes' dreary tramping (Mont Blanc is all a dreary tramp, except for the last few hundred yards) brought us to the end of the tracks which the guides had made the night before. There we stopped and put on our skis. Without them we sank into the snow well above our knees.

This was the first time that any of us had worn skis for nearly six months, and, except for Georges, we were all pretty clumsy on them at the start. Every movement that he made was graceful, and you could have seen in a moment that he was a born ski champion (he is champion of the world in one of the long distance ski events!).

The snow was very soft and powdery, so we had to make long zigzags to keep from slipping backwards as we went up. Even with the zigzags, almost all my weight came on the ski-poles in my hands. My arms were the first part of my body to get tired from this new exercise.

We had scarcely put on our skis when we came to a huge, black, yawning cavern with a ladder over it. They had to be all undone and taken off so that we could climb the ladder. And then we had to put them on again above it. It was an awful bother just to cross a gap ten feet wide.

The upper "lip" of this crevasse was so much higher than the lower one, that the guides said it would be safe to jump it with skis on the way down. I formed my opinion at once—NOT FOR ME! A little later, the rest decided likewise.

The climb was, for me, much like that of a year ago. Georges went ahead with a lantern and Cachat was behind me; then came Antoine and Sherry. There was always the thump, thump of Georges ahead and Cachat behind, and always the flicker of the lantern on the snow. We climbed for so long like that that I nearly fell asleep with the monotony of it.

An hour above the ladder we came to the edge of what is called the "Petit Plateau," a great plain of flat snow, lying just below the Grand Plateau. Just below the plateau the snow was very hard, because the wind had swept off the new-fallen, soft snow. Also it was so steep that we could not make any zigzags, and we had to "side-step" for a couple of hundred feet. Side-stepping is going up sideways. You first lift one ski and then you lift the other one up beside it. Then, if you do it all over again, and keep it up until you nearly fall in a heap, you go two hundred feet!

Those two hundred feet were absolutely the most tiring part of the whole trip, because we had to use exactly the same muscles over and over again, till they were just plain worn out.

We crossed the Petit Plateau at a good stiff pace. Then, after zigzagging up another slope we reached the Grand Plateau, where we stopped to rest for a moment.

Georges had extinguished the lantern on the Petit Plateau and put it in his sack, for, from there on, we had had light enough to see our way. Now it was really light and the sun had just risen.

Down below in the valley of Chamonix the lights twinkled brightly, since it was still only four in the morning. As far as I could see, everything was a gorgeous red. It was just like the sunrise I had had on the Grand Plateau a year before and I just revelled in it.

The evening mists still surged around in the valley and, far to the south, a heavy bank of black clouds could be seen, slowly advancing toward us. All the signs pointed to bad weather—especially the very red sunrise.

Mont Blanc itself was right ahead of us, and I saw Sherry scanning it with a crestfallen eye. From end to end of the ridge by which we must climb it raced a terrific wind. The new snow, which had lain so peacefully for a couple of days, was whipped into furious eddies by the blast and swirled along at a stupendous speed.

Just then an icy gust struck me full in the face and nearly blew me over with its force. It was the morning wind that we had feared. Mont Blanc would be impossible.

Sherry saw the situation at once and decided that he would return, and not bother to climb any longer, now that the hopes for the summit were all gone. So he and Antoine turned about and started off downwards, disappearing in a few moments over the rim of the Plateau.

Cachat, Georges, and I planned to make an attempt to reach the Col du Dôme, the lowest point on the ridge between Mont Blanc and the Dôme du Goûter, in order to get a few pictures of the wind-swept crest of Mont Blanc.

We lingered talking so long that Georges got his whole left foot frost-bitten, and he had to kick it violently for a few minutes to get it so that he could walk on it once more. Then we set off as fast as we could go for the Col du Dôme.

The difference in altitude between the Grand Plateau and the valley was now very definite. I breathed in short quick gasps, and whenever I exerted myself at all, it made me puff and blow terribly. There was very little oxygen in the air, for, as you know, it gets less and less dense as you go on upward from sealevel.

The climbing was easy enough in that dreadful, thin air if I advanced very evenly and smoothly, but the moment I made a sudden movement, I had to stop and rest for a minute to get back my strength.

The slope of the Col du Dôme got less and less steep, and finally we emerged on the great ridge which leads unbroken to the summit of Mont Blanc. In good weather conditions, we could have got to the summit in two more tedious hours. But now it was hopeless. Georges' foot was worse instead of better, as he had expected it would be. Now Cachat had got a frozen hand. The wind was crossing the ridge furiously, carrying with it a heavy load of snow. In fact, the snow was blowing around in such thick clouds that it looked like a real snow-storm, although the sky was absolutely blue above our heads!

The wind would whip the snow from the level fields, swirl it into the air, race it up the side of Mont Blanc in a perfect tempest, and then it would cross the ridge and rush out into the air in tremendous white clouds. It was an awe-inspiring sight.

You can look at the picture of Mont Blanc and see where the

little shack of the Vallot Refuge is situated. Then you can find the rocks above the Corridor. To give some idea of the speed of that wind, it was racing from the Refuge to those rocks in less than five seconds! No human being could long stand up against *that*.

Even where we were, it was so violent that we could actually lean up against it without falling down. Try that yourself some day against a stiff wind, and you'll find that it has to blow nearly seventy miles an hour before you can do it.

In the midst of all that inferno of wind and flying snow, I actually managed to change a film in my camera. And I got some pictures without freezing my hands, while the guides were standing by freezing up tight! It takes a lot to freeze me, but, I must admit that I just go flat on my back when it gets really hot.

I took four pictures and then gave the camera to Cachat to put away in his sack. Just as I was handing it to him, one of my gloves which I had had off while taking the pictures blew right away. Luckily it was, at that moment, a lull between two blasts of wind, and Cachat made one leap with his skis and slid down to it. This pulled the rope around my waist up tight and pitched me on my ear in the soft snow!

I got up and wrung the icy snow off my gloveless hand—it's terrible to get your hand wet in a place as cold as that. Then I turned about and looked at Georges. As usual the little demon (he is a good three inches shorter than I am) was laughing at me. I couldn't see anything funny in it at all. It reminded me of my first time in the Mummery Crack, when I had got my foot stuck and he had pulled me.

His laughing was silenced by an icy gust of wind, which caught me full in the face and nearly bowled me over. The weather was steadily growing worse. Great wreaths of snow were swirling up from the rocks of the Vallot Refuge just above us on the ridge. It was time to go, or we might never go. I thought of the three skiers who had been lost on this ridge last winter, and whose frozen bodies had been found but ten days before!

Georges unroped me so fast that I could not explain to him about my glove through the roar of the wind. A swirl of snow lost Cachat to my view for a moment. He was about twenty feet below me, waiting with the glove. I made a little jump turn, and started slipping towards him to get it. Just above him, I struck an icy spot on top of the snow, and away I went a million miles an hour—past Cachat, and down the slope toward the Grand Plateau.

It hadn't seemed steep on the way up, but going down—Whew! The snow seemed to fly before me. I was going with the wind and I served as a sort of a sail for myself as I tore at lightning speed down that half-mile slope.

It was the most difficult snow imaginable to stand up on. Here and there were patches of crust over which I raced like fury. Then I would strike soft snow again, and slow up like a shot. I managed to keep my balance until I had reached the upper edge of the Grand Plateau. I had never gone so fast on skis before, and knew my end was soon in store for me. Zoom—a patch of ice—a patch of snow—THEN. I rose gently into the air in a graceful curve and, after a twenty-foot dive, I landed right on my head in the snow. For what seemed like hours I rolled and rolled, head over heels down the gradual slope of the plateau. It was a wonder that my skis didn't break my ankles and turn them to pulp.

Finally I came to a stop upside down, and up to my hips in the soft snow. The wind was simply terrific. When I managed to extricate myself and straighten up, I found that one of the skis had come loose a little and that I would have to take it off again to adjust it. I took off my one remaining glove for the operation. When it was fixed and on once more, I located Georges through the clouds of flying snow. He was on the lower edge of the plateau, and another sensational slide and spill took me to him.

Even the ski champions like Georges and Cachat were spilling. The snow was just wrong for any kind of turn or stop except for those which I had been patronizing. When I reached Georges and got up on my feet again, Cachat was at least a quarter of a mile behind me with my glove in his pocket, and fixing his ski which had come off. My left hand, the gloveless one, was now completely *black* from the wrist to the ends of the fingers. I could no longer feel anything that I touched with it.

That blackness is the first stage of freezing. I was sure of it and was just mad to get my glove. Georges, too, was eager to get started for both his feet were in bad condition. At last Cachat came and I put the glove on. It was full of ice which the wind had blown into it when it fell, but I couldn't feel it at all. By the time I had got it on again, the others had disappeared through the mist of fine snow that was flying through the air. I waited for a moment to find them and then started off.

The snow got a little more powdery on the way to the Petit Plateau, and by making long, gentle zigzags with skid stops at their ends, we managed to descend very rapidly. In the soft snow, too, the poles were very handy, as we could use them for brakes by placing them between our legs and sitting on them! This drove the points deep into the snow, and we could stop that way whenever we wanted to.

With bamboo ski-poles this is a very dangerous thing to do, because they are apt to break and hurt you very badly. Luckily we had poles made of little saplings, and they were very strong and safe.

All the way across the Petit Plateau and down the steep slopes to the crevasse with the ladder, the storm of blowing snow raged unceasingly, often getting so thick that I couldn't see either of the guides. If I stopped for a moment to get my breath, the tracks that they had made filled level with the blowing snow. It was a really exciting adventure—a true storm on the highest peak in Europe, and on skis too!

It was an awful job crossing the crevasse with the ladder and putting on our skis again on the other side of it. Now I could see the Grands Mulets between the gusts of wind and snow. The guides were getting slowly farther ahead, but they couldn't go very fast on account of the extremely steep grade, and the large number of crevasses which yawned on all sides of us. I would go tearing down a slope and stop at the very edge of a crevasse. Then a kick turn would start me back on another zigzag, running lengthwise between two more crevasses.

Turn after turn and zigzags by the million brought me to a little rise just above the Grands Mulets. The spot was sheltered by a massive wall of séracs that towered above me, and the storm had at last ceased. Of course, there was a hurricane of wind where I was, but I had got lower than the region of soft snow. The snow here had melted the day before and had frozen into a hard crust, so the wind raced across it harmlessly. But it was now too dangerous to continue on skis, for the little slope that lay between me and the Grands Mulets was all in glare ice. So I took my skis off, and, tying them together again, I shouldered them and started off on the run, steadying myself with a pole in my left hand.

Ten minutes later we were all together before the warm fire at the hut. Georges had had his hand frost-bitten, and Cachat had nearly frozen a hand and one of his feet. My hand had really been the worst of the three injured parts. It had, however, been saved by a miracle. If you have a part of you freezing, queer to say, the only way to stop it is to cover it with snow or ice! The ice that had saved my left hand was what had gotten in my glove when Cachat had fallen while bringing it to me on the Grand Plateau!

When I was all warm again, I went out and looked at Mont Blanc from a sheltered corner among the rocks behind the hut. The wind was sweeping along the final cone of the mountain at a stupendous rate, probably nearly two hundred miles an hour! Wisps of snow went whirling up into the brilliant blue sky in much the same way that we had seen them from the Col du Dôme but much smaller and less terrible.

There's nothing like the game in which you match yourself against Nature. Give her your very best and fight to the end, but when you see that she has got the upper hand, turn, and don't be scared to admit defeat. It's the fool who sticks to it when it's impossible. A real alpinist always turns when he feels that the time has come—he's praised more, sometimes, for his sense in turning back than when he reaches the top. And, after all, there's nothing like the feeling of knowing that you've done your best, even though you've lost in the struggle!

Tightening Up Packs at the Five-Mile Post.

BRADFORD ON MOUNT WASHINGTON

BY

BRADFORD WASHBURN

ILLUSTRATED WITH PHOTOGRAPHS TAKEN BY
THE AUTHOR, MAURICE KELLERMANN, AND OTHERS

This book is dedicated
to the memory of my Uncle Charles,
whose great kindness has made possible
my climbing in the Alps.

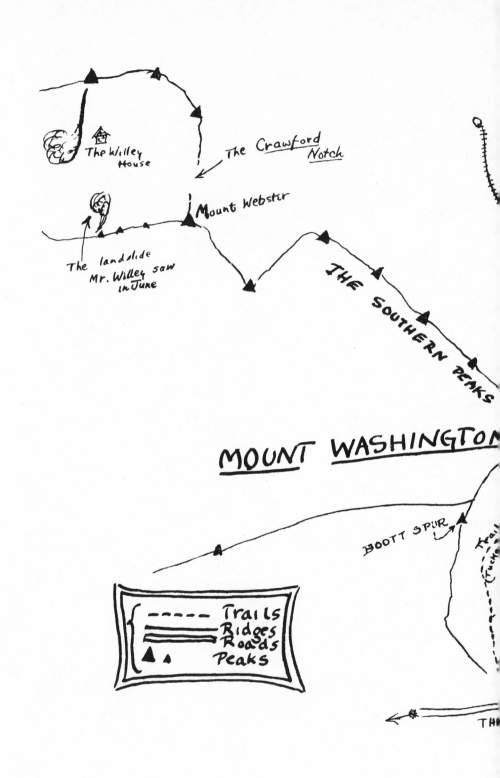

The Willey House

The Crawford Notch

Mount Webster

The landslide Mr. Willey saw in June

THE SOUTHERN PEAKS

MOUNT WASHINGTON

BOOTT SPUR

Trail (Tucke...

{ ----- Trails
≡≡≡ Ridges
Roads
▲ ▴ Peaks

TH...

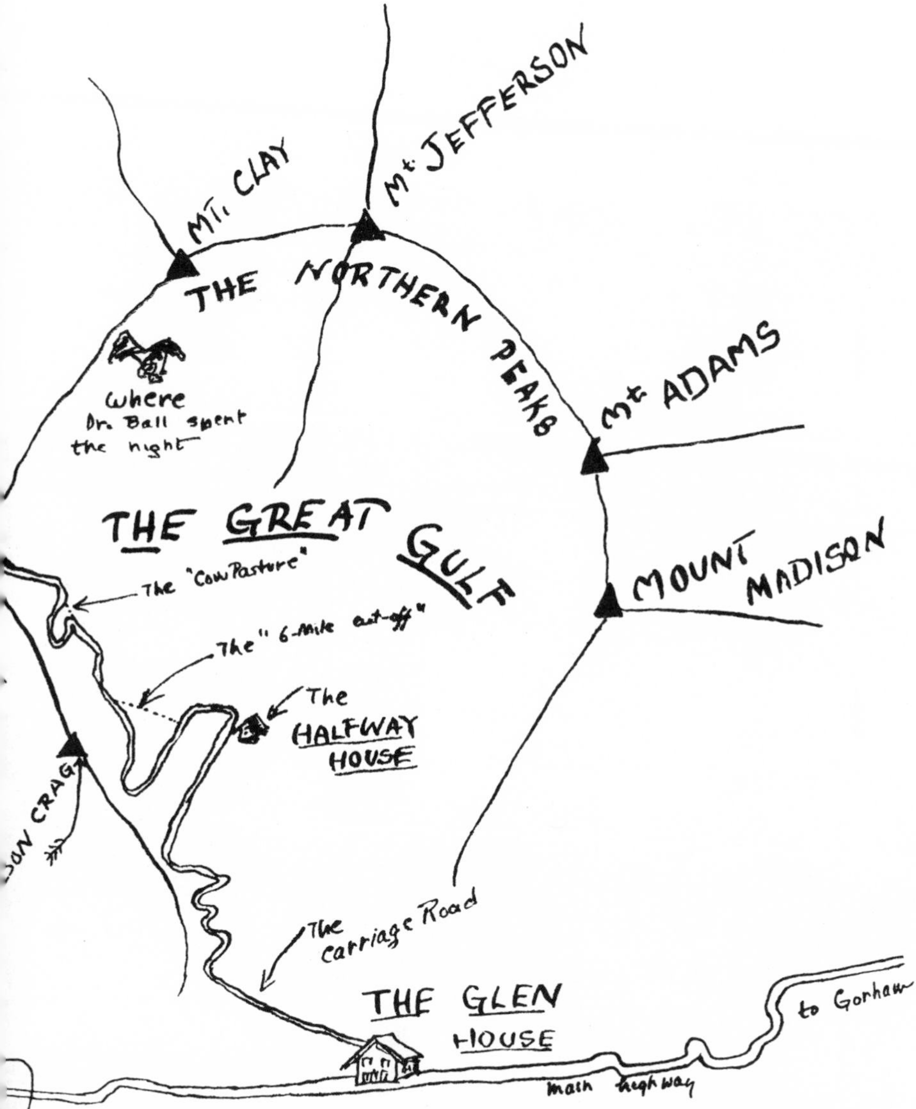
Mt. CLAY
Mt. JEFFERSON
THE NORTHERN PEAKS
Mt. ADAMS
where Dr. Ball spent the night
THE GREAT GULF
MOUNT MADISON
The "Cow Pasture"
The "6-Mile cut-off"
The HALFWAY HOUSE
The carriage Road
THE GLEN HOUSE
to Gorham
main highway
NOTCH

CONTENTS

PHOTOGRAPHS

PREFACE

Two successive summers in the Alps make a rather high standard of thrills up to which to pull the White Mountains of New Hampshire. But I have know the White Hills intimately for the past six years. I have lived in them and on them and have got to know them from end to end. And I have found out with very little difficulty that Mount Washington in a bad mood can furnish as many exciting moments as Mont Blanc.

The trouble with the White Mountains is that far too few people really know them in their angry, alpine state. In winter during the months between December and April it seems as though the slopes of Mt. Washington were transported to Switzerland. Wild gales sweep the upper ridges of the mountain and its neighboring peaks. Terrific snowstorms fill the ravines to depths of over one hundred feet. Jack Frost reigns supreme on "The Range" for five months every year.

The remainder of the year always sees thousands of camp girls and boys climb the easy slopes of the mountain to attain the summit of the highest peak on New England. The view from Mount Washington is unsurpassed in all the East. In fact, just a week ago I saw a mountain nearly a hundred miles away to the south and one can see the Atlantic Ocean fully eighty miles to the East in very good weather.

It is for those sturdy Americans who are interested in mountaineering, the greatest of all sports, that this book is written. It is for those who like to venture into the gales and snow, and for those who like to battle nature on her own wide slopes and crags.

—B. W.

CHAPTER I

EARLY EXPLORERS
AND SETTLERS

The White Mountains are a wide-spread group mostly of hills running from the border between Massachusetts and New Hampshire, northward almost into Canada. The mountains stretch the whole width of the state. They are, however, small with one or two exceptions. In the extreme southern part Monadnock and Kearsarge rise to heights of three thousand feet and slightly over. Just north of the middle of the state lies the Great Range—the Presidential Range. The mountains of this group lie in a series of ridges like the spokes of a wheel, all leading to Mount Washington. This mountain, the highest in New England, is six thousand two hundred and eighty-seven feet in height. Its last two and a half thousand feet are almost absolutely bare rock. A shrub grows here and there and clumps of grass are found even near the top of the mountain. A great broad shoulder of the peak which is almost flat is called the Alpine Garden. Flowers grow there, many of which appear only on that spot and in the Alps.

Mount Washington is about three hundred feet higher than Mount Adams, the next highest of "The Range." Then the other peaks string out in order.

Due mostly to their being so much higher than all the rest of the New Hampshire mountains, the Presidentials were worshiped by the Indians. They thought that the Great Spirit and all of the other spirits of good and evil dwelt way up there in the clouds, and they feared that they would be killed by the spirits if they ventured near their homes.

The Indians being a very superstitious race must have found it very easy to believe that the mountains were enchanted. The thunderstorms and squalls that arise on the peaks of the Presidentials are the most severe that I have ever seen anywhere. A blue sky without a cloud in sight can turn into lightning, thunder, and rain in ten or fifteen minutes and sometimes even less.

In June 1642, Darby Field, an Irishman living at Exeter, New Hampshire, made the first known trip up Mount Washington. He was accompanied to a point within eight miles of the summit by a large group of Indians. At that point the Indians said that they refused to go an inch further. They entreated Field to stop and not go on himself for he might never come back alive.

The explorer, however, challenged anyone to come on with him and set out up the peak. Two Indian youths separated from the group and said that they would stick by him. The day was clear and rather cool and they found no difficulty in reaching the top of Mount Washington by a route which is unknown to us today, although it was probably by Boott Spur. (See the map.)

The three men saw heaps of snow that the summer's heat had not yet melted. They went through a number of clouds on the way up and finally got to the top quite exhausted. They looked down into the "Great Gulf" which lies between Mount Washington and the Northern peaks and claimed it so deep that they could scarcely see its bottom.

A short stay on top was enough for them and they returned to the Indians' camp in the valley. The whole company was surprised to see them again and said that during their absence a fierce thunderstorm had made them think that the mountain spirits were finishing them off!

After Mount Washington had been climbed it suffered a like fate to that of Mont Blanc after its conquest. Between 1642 and about 1800 the range was traveled now and then, but not very frequently. Around the beginning of the Nineteenth Century, however, the mountain country was very well peopled and such families as the Willeys and the Crawfords began to make themselves well known.

The Crawfords were a family who lived some eight miles from the top of Mount Washington on the west side. Most of their famous work was the building of the Bridle Path up Mount Washington along the eight-mile ridge of the Southern Peaks and the establishment of the first little hut on top for sheltering the adventurous tourists who went up the mountain by their new trail. This path was completed in 1816. In 1826 an accident and tragedy occurred which has been the heart of many stories connected with the White Mountains. The Willey House Tragedy is to the White Mountains what the Whymper tragedy on the Matterhorn is to the Alps.

The Crawford Notch (see the map) lies about ten miles to the southwest of Mount Washington at the most southern extremity of the Southern Peaks. In 1793 a Mr. Davis erected a house at the bottom of this deep declivity between the ranges of four thousand foot peaks. He called it the Notch House. It was in a most fearfully lonely spot, five or six miles from where the Crawfords lived at the head of the Notch and about the same distance from the nearest settlement to the south.

The Notch House was put up merely for an inn and refreshment house for travelers, making their way up through the mountains, and especially for winter travelers. The house was too lonely for Davis and also for Hill his successor, so in 1825 it was abandoned. Samuel Willey of Bartlett moved in and took control of the house in the fall of 1825 with two hired men, his wife, and five children.

During that fall and winter the house was run beautifully. The guests came, were cared for, and left. Nothing out of the usual train of events took place. One afternoon in June, Mr. and Mrs. Willey were sitting on the porch. A thunderstorm had passed and the mountains were as still as death. Suddenly, as they talked and watched the slopes of Mount Webster across the little narrow valley, they heard a roar. A great clot of earth or a boulder seemed to be moving downwards nearly at the crest of Webster's Ridge.

The clot grew larger and larger, leaving a deep scar behind it. The noise grew louder and finally a great cascade of rocks, dirt, sand, and splintered trees roared into the brook in the valley. There were a few echoes and then silence reigned again, except for the rumbling of thunder in the distance.

As Mr. and Mrs. Willey looked at each other in amazement and horror another but smaller slide roared away into the valley. Mr. Willey was all for leaving the spot at once and seeking a safer place for their family. But the next day it was clear and no slide occurred. The family gradually forgot the experience and it faded away into the past.

All summer long there was a great drought. The ground grew drier and drier. The dirt was baked as hard as rock. The roots became stiff with the heat and lack of water.

Late in the afternoon of Monday, August 28, Mr. Benjamin Willey, Samuel's brother was returning to his home in Bartlett. He happened to look over his shoulder and was amazed at the dark, heavy, billowy clouds that were collecting over the Mount Washington Range. When he got home he looked up in the Crawford Notch direction and again noticed the very heavy accumulation of clouds over the mountain. He was tired after a long drive and went to bed early, sleeping like a log.

Rain started to fall at sunset and kept on falling heavily for a few hours. At midnight Mr. Willey's brother heard the stable door slam and as he rounded the corner of the house going out to latch it again, he saw a strange sight.

The storm was over and the stars were all shining brilliantly. Over the Presidential Range hung a dark curtain of clouds. It covered every peak completely. Out of this thick blanket Mr. Willey saw a terrific display of lightning which lit up the whole sky. There was not a single sound of thunder.

He went to bed only to be wakened again in an hour or so to go down to the intervales along the Saco River. The Saco had overflowed its banks and sheep were being drowned in the low-lying fields. By breakfast most of the sheep had been driven to safety. The river had in seven hours risen a vertical height of twenty-four feet! The storm through which Mr. Willey had slept had been the greatest ever known to White Mountain history, that of last November ranking a rather poor second.

All this happened on Monday night. Tuesday night a traveler from the Crawfords came to Bartlett to say that Mr. Samuel Willey's whole family had been wiped out up in the notch. Mr. Willey's brother and sister-in-law thought this a practical joke, but the next evening another voyager confirmed the report.

On Wednesday, directly after the second report, Mr. Willey and his wife and brother-in-law set out for the Notch House through the scenes of washout and destruction that the storm had left in its wake. When they reached the Notch House clearing a horrible wreck met their eyes. Piles of huge trees, splintered like match-wood and stripped of their bark lay on every side. A great gouge rent the side of the peak that is now called Mount Willey, begin-ning a few hundred yards from the top and ending in the Saco at the bottom of the valley.

The Notch House remained intact, but its barn was gone, swept away by the gigantic landslide. In the house were evidences of a sudden departure. A Bible lay open on the table and clothes were scattered around the room. A hard search of the debris around the remains of the barn revealed all of the bodies except those of the children. These have never been found.

The only plausible explanation for the tragic episode is that which has been told to one of Mr. Willey's brothers by Mr. Willey's ghost in a dream some days after the accident. In the dream Mr. Willey's brother asked him why he and his family fled the house to their deaths. The ghost answered that the water had risen so high in the intervales that he was afraid that the house might be swept away. So they all fled to a little rise behind the barn and it was there that the slide met and carried them away. The landslide split in two over a knoll behind the house, one half passing on each side. It was one of these streams of rocks that buried the barn near which the family had taken shelter.

It is a weird way for an explanation of the accident to be revealed, but of all the ideas anybody advanced after the tragedy this is far and away the most plausible. It was the greatest disaster that the White Mountains have ever known.

CHAPTER II

A DOCTOR HAS DIFFICULTIES

As I said back in the introduction, winter is the time to visit Mount Washington. Before I tell of my trips up the peak in winter, I want to write a few words on the experiences of a Boston doctor on the mountain as well as telling of the interesting and exciting work of the United States weather men in a little observatory on top of Mount Washington in the winters between 1871 and 1887.

Twenty-four years (1855) after the Willey landslide a Dr. Ball of Boston decided that he wanted to make the ascent of Mount Washington. The time of year he chose was not the best by any means. Late October and early November are usually very cold on the range. Little if any snow has fallen, but the rocks are covered deep in a coating of frost feathers, making the going extremely difficult.

Clear weather seemed to be the forecast, so Dr. Ball left Boston for Gorham, New Hampshire, by way of Portland, Maine. At Gorham, where he arrived early one morning at the end of October, he learned that the only way to see the mountains well in the cloudy weather they were having would be to go on to the Glen House. So Dr. Ball took a suitcase, an umbrella, and a horse, and strapping the suitcase to the saddle he rode in to the Glen.

The Glen is at the very foot of Mount Washington and is the

The Pinkham Notch Camp and Mount Washington.

place where the Carriage Road up the mountains begins. At that time, however, the road was completed only to a little beyond the four mile point (it is now eight miles long) and had been staked from there to the top.

When Dr. Ball arrived at the Glen the weather didn't look at all forbidding, so he left the hotel situated there with a warning from the proprietor not to go any farther up than where the road workmen were unless the weather became absolutely clear.

Leaving his suitcase at the Glen and taking his umbrella to shield him from a drizzling rain that had commenced, Dr. Ball made the first four miles of the road in two hours. He continued up the bridle path and staked out road which led to the top. He safely passed the cabin where the workmen spent the night and climbed over a heap of rock known as "The Ledge."

A short distance above the ledge, the doctor encountered a severe wind and cold with sleet and rain. So he turned about and made for the workmen's cabin. There he spent the night with the men and the next morning he started out on his way up the mountain once more.

The weather was still unsettled. Heavy clouds hung over the peaks and hid them from view. The wind was blowing rather hard and the air was full of misty rain. He pressed on up the bridle path which got fainter and fainter as he climbed, till finally he lost both it and the line of stakes in the dense fog.

He got to the top of what he called the "first mountain" (probably Nelson Crag, see the map) by a struggle into the wind and rain. The going grew easier and then harder until he reached the top of the "third mountain" where a violent snowstorm was raging. From there he thought that he could see the top of Mount Washington. He hastened on, his hands and feet growing colder and colder in spite of his heavy boots borrowed at the camp that morning.

A really hard fight got him to the "top" of the mountain. There the land appeared flat for a bit and then to slope downward on all sides. I have no doubt whatsoever that this spot is a crag that rises out of an almost level field of rock just below the top of Mount Washington. In a heavy fog one might easily mistake it for the top except for the absence of buildings.

Poor Dr. Ball was in a bad fix. All the land about him seemed to go downward, yet where was the Summit House? Where was the warm fire promised him by the road workers that morning? The wind buffeted him harder and harder as he looked about for signs of habitation. None were visible anywhere. He found a big overhanging rock and sat down beneath it to decide what to do.

Even a moment's rest began to make him feel sleepy, the fatal first step to freezing to death, so he got up and started to descend. The wind and snow lashed him even more fiercely than before. Finally he found the stakes once more. It was too late to start climbing, so he hurried along their line. Some short scrubby trees ahead announced the treeline and then, abruptly, the stakes stopped, leaving him bewildered at the edge of a dense section of thick undergrowth.

Night was coming on so he hurried in a search for a rock under which to spend it. He found one quite near the scrub line and between it and some low spruces he rigged up a sort of shelter out of boughs of trees and his umbrella.

By squirming, talking out loud, and putting himself in crazy positions, he succeeded in getting through the night without a single touch of the death-bearing sleep. It was a wonder that the wind, too, didn't carry away his umbrella. This was a godsend without which he would have died before an hour of the night passed.

He had a conference with himself in which he decided first to look for the stakes that he had lost the night before. In case he couldn't find these he would encircle the mountain keeping at the same altitude. Thus he would be sure to strike his route of ascent the day before.

He couldn't find the stakes so he began his encircling job. Four hours of this brought him no good. Then he turned and stumbled back to the rock where he had spent the night. Just as he was reaching the rock he heard a sound of voices and a noise of feet. He turned and there at some distance on a little cliff of rock stood two men. He tried to yell to them, but his voice choked because of lack of water. He waved and they didn't seem to notice him. Were they rocks? No, they turned suddenly and disappeared in the clouds!

Dr. Ball could do nothing but return to his rock and make over his shelter with the umbrella and branches. He spent another night there even more terrible than the first with the snow drifting in about him and the wind tearing at his precious umbrella.

At last daylight came and he set out again to find a way down. A little after he started he saw a house down in the valley through a vista in the clouds. He was so tired that he rested nearly two hours on a wide rock before moving on again. When he did he was rewarded. Just ahead of him he saw a group of men looking at the foot-deep snow. They seemed to be picking out a trail. He squawked at them, for this was the best that he could do! Then he waved. The men saw him and, dumbfounded, they came forward and asked him why he was alive. The only reason was his terrific persistence. It was lucky that he hadn't climbed what he thought to be Mount Washington the day before. It was Mount Jefferson three miles to the northeast of Washington!

The men who had been sent from the road-workers camp were just about to give up the search as they had done the day before, when Dr. Ball had seen them on the little cliff. Dr. Ball survived his experience, but suffered many months from frost-bitten feet and hands and the other results of exposure which probably will never be equaled except for the case of Max Englehart. He lived for three days with a dislocated hip in the snows of Tuckerman Ravine, dragged himself for a half mile, and was rescued by Joe Dodge of Pinkham Notch and one of his companions, after many, many hours on the mountain.

Nearly twenty years after Dr. Ball's experience on the range the United States Government established a meteorological survey (weather station) on the summit of Mount Washington. It was kept steadily for sixteen years (1871–1887) summer and winter, and during the summer for a few years after that. Among the wonderful things done by this commission was the fixing of a world's record for wind velocity—184 miles an hour!

To give you some idea of the storms that those men went through on the summit and also to prove that Mount Washington in winter is as fierce as the Alps, I am going to write a few of the happenings that occurred during one of their storms.

In January 1877, the greatest storm on record occurred. The thermometer dropped steadily all day till it was 21 degrees below Zero at sunset with the wind at 90 miles an hour. During the night the temperature got lower and lower till it had dropped to 51 degrees below Zero with the wind at 184 miles an hour just before sunrise. The boards were blown from the windows and it took both observers and a wooden lever to push and jam them back into place again. Water froze three feet from a red hot stove and the men later admitted that they were all ready to be blown down the mountain. They had, for safety, in case the hut blew away, bound themselves tightly with quilts, blankets, sacks, and pillows and tied crowbars to this rig before they tried to sleep, so that they might not get blown quite so far and hit so hard if they blew away!

These were the stories that we had heard and this was the mountain that we planned to climb when we started our preparations two years ago Christmas.

THE PEAK IN WINTER

In 1925 I made my first winter visit to Mount Washington. During the last two years I had made a number of summer ascents of the mountain and had grown to love it in its quiet, peaceful state, although I had already been caught in two violent thunderstorms on its ridges.

Our first climbing party stayed at Gorham, New Hampshire, some ten miles from the mountain and eight miles from the Glen House. The Glen House gets its name from its situation in a deep valley between the Carter and Mount Washington Ranges. It lies on a slope of the Carter Range, about two hundred yards from the Peabody River and directly facing Mount Washington. The Northern Peaks and Mount Washington rise in a tremendous amphitheatre before the Glen House as do the Aiguilles and Mont Blanc about Chamonix.

I will never forget the feeling that I had when I first saw Mount Washington in winter. A few miles north of the Glen we were coming along the snow-drifted road in an auto. I was amazed at the marvelous beauty of the trees and the frozen cataracts of the Peabody River which flowed on our right. Every branch was laden nearly to breaking with a deep covering of snow and the bright, sparkling water of the river occasionally showed up through thin, transparent spots in the ice.

Then Dave Crocker, my companion, cried out, "There it is!" I looked up, and there it was. Mount Washington rose at the end of the valley, a mass of pure white snow and glittering ice. Above the treeline, which is at about 4,000 feet on that side of the mountain, all was white. Nothing stuck through the smooth banks of snow, some nearly a mile long, except a few big rocks here and there.

I was terribly surprised by the sight, I had expected to see a slightly whitened summer Mount Washington. This was a regular Alp! It was a gorgeously brilliant day; this first view of Mount Washington at Christmas leaves a perfect picture of the snowy peak in my mind.

We returned the eight miles to Gorham that evening after getting views all day as wonderful as this first. The next day, Father, my brother Sherry, Dave, and I took a "leg-stretcher" up to the Halfway House on the Carriage Road. The Carriage Road leads from the Glen to the top of Mount Washington and is eight miles long. The following day the good weather prevailed, so Dave and I tried to climb to the top by the Carriage Road. But we got a late start and by three o'clock in the afternoon we had only reached the five-mile post. So we turned and went beck to the Glen.

Another good day had been wasted and we were disappointed with our luck. As we had feared, bad weather set in and it snowed for two days. On the third day it stopped snowing and the clouds lifted to the Halfway House. We *must* make our attempt to get up to the top for we had to go the next day. So we set out from Pinkham Notch, three miles south of the Glen (the opposite direction from Gorham), at eight o'clock in the morning.

We climbed up through the woods which were buried under nearly six feet of snow. The Tuckerman Ravine trail led us up to Hermit Lake, a tiny desolate pool of water two miles above Pinkham. There we had a wonderful view of the great ravine which rises a thousand feet above the little pond in two steep slopes. The second slope (the "Headwall") is almost a cliff in summer and a waterfall courses down its face. In winter the snows are blown over the cliff from the great smooth expanses of the mountain above and fill this gigantic hole to a depth of over a hundred feet.

Hermit Lake and Tuckerman Ravine.

Base of the Headwall, Tuckerman Ravine, in a Snowstorm. Left to Right:
G. P. Putnam, the Author, Waters Kellogg, Fred Seibert, Dick Hodges.

When the ravine is filled deep with this blanket of snow, the
Headwall is a wonderful climb for somebody out for exciting
Alpine work. The rocks are nearly covered by the hard snow
which has been packed and drifted in by the wind and the cliff is
a smooth fifty-degree slope. Once at the top of this great slope, a
thousand more feet of much less steep climbing along the snow-
covered rocks brings you to the top of the mountain. This last
steady slope above the Headwall is called the "cone" of Mount
Washington.

The deep snow was very powdery for a good distance above
Hermit Lake until we got over the first steep slope and above the
treeline at the base of the main headwall. Here we got out our ice-
axes and began to cut the large number of steps necessary to get
us up the Headwall and to the foot of the cone (about a thousand
feet).

Halfway up the Headwall we went into the clouds, but it wasn't
cold enough to feel chilled by them. The thermometer was about
twenty degrees. It was our first taste of steep snow climbing and
Dave and I got a bit nervous as we neared the top of the great

gully and looked down the thousand-foot cliff, watching the chunks of ice and hard snow from our steps as they bounded away to its bottom.

At noon we reached the base of the cone and after a short rest we continued upward through heavy fog, swept along by a twenty-mile breeze. It got colder and colder as we went up and we heaved a sigh of relief as we opened the door of Camden Cottage. The cottage is a little one-story twelve-foot-by-eighteen-foot shack on top of the mountain. It was built to shelter people who climb in winter and also to keep these climbers from breaking into the larger buildings on top, which are open only in summer. Patrick Camden, an employee of the Boston and Maine Railroad for many years, was the person who had most to do with the erection of the little cabin.

Our stay on top was short. We got there at 12:45 and left about one o'clock. Our trip down, too, is of little interest. You see, the Carriage Road is the safest way down in winter and is nothing but an eight-mile, snow-covered road. However, the views from the road are marvelous and on the way down we went through two layers of clouds and could see for miles over tossing billows of misty clouds that lay below us.

My first trip up Mount Washington was a great success. That March in our Easter vacation, Tappey Turner, a Groton friend of mine, and I made another trip by Tuckerman Ravine (the really sporty way to do the peak in winter). Ray Evans of Gorham was our guide and he certainly earned what he got for his work.

The Headwall of Tuckerman had a tremendous amount of snow on it, so we decided to climb right up its middle. It got steeper and steeper. Evans had an ice-axe and Tappey and I each had a three-foot stick of pine cut near Hermit Lake. We helped ourselves along with the sticks and steadied ourselves in the steps which Evans cut.

An unusual lot of snow had drifted down to Hermit Lake were it lay some *twenty feet* on the level, almost hiding the trees. From the lake to the Headwall was a terrible fight through drifts and branches because the summer's trail, which had still been visible at Christmas, was hidden far below us under the snow.

At last we reached the Headwall where the smooth brick-hard snow covered everything. Then we tried on our "crampons" (spikes for the bottoms of your shoes). The first half of the well-packed but very steep slope we made easily in a half hour. Then the fun began.

What had looked like the top of the cliff from the bottom was really nothing but a ledge that hid from view the other slope above us! Difficulties piled up right and left. On top of the hard snow in which we were cutting our steps was a layer of soft snow. A hundred weary feet further up we found a crust on the soft snow and then another layer of soft snow on that. To make every step Evans had to smash and sweep away these upper layers, get to the hard snow, and there do his cutting.

It was a terribly tedious job and Evans kept turning back at Tappey and me to say, "Gorry, it's hot, boys!" Then he would turn back to his work again, leaving Tappey and me in the steps he had just cut, nearly freezing to death from lack of exercise!

In a couple of places Evans was forced to cut diagonal trenches in the soft snow up which we crawled on our hands and knees. Here our sticks were very handy to keep us from slipping back.

Four hours and twenty minutes after we had begun at the base of the headwall we stopped to rest at the lower edge of the cone. That made it four-thirty in the afternoon and far too late to go on, so we traversed the east side of the cone until we reached the Carriage Road about a mile from the top of the mountain. The day had given us poor weather as the summit was in the clouds and had been all afternoon, but it was not very cold. The temperature had proved just comfortable for climbing, except on the Headwall where Tappey and I had not been able to get our blood stirring much.

We reached the Halfway House at six o'clock and had a hasty supper in the shed. We hadn't eaten since eleven o'clock at Hermit Lake. We got to the Glen two hours later after a descent on snowshoes along the road in the pitch dark.

Last Christmas (1926) saw us there, and this winter (1927) we had a big trip. Mr. Putnam, the publisher of this book, came up with Maurice Kellerman, his cameraman, and, despite terrible

Hermit Lake Shelter, Christmas 1927.

luck on weather, we got a lot of good photographs, many of which you see in this book. We stayed three nights in Camden Cottage and came down by way of Tuckerman Ravine without seeing a view once on account of the heavy low-lying clouds.

The thrill of that trip—every trip seems to have some special thrill—was my spending a night alone with Kelly (Mr. Kellerman) in the Hermit Lake Shelter, a few hundred yards from Hermit Lake.

Mr. Putman and some of my friends, Dick Hodges, Ed Hall, Fredrick Seibert, and Waters Kellogg helped Kelly and me to put a tarpaulin on half of the front of the little three-sided log shelter. Then they loaded the wall with snow on which they heaved water. This made the shelter pretty well wind proof.

While this was going on Kelly took still pictures and movies of the work and I cut up wood for the fire. At about five in the afternoon they left us alone, as they all had to go to Boston and New York for various reasons.

Just after they left the wind began to tune up—directly into the open half of our cabin! By twisting the "tarp" we arranged a little corner big enough for our sleeping bags (six of them!). Then we

Brad Cooks Some Bacon at the Shelter.

had supper as it was beginning to get dark; pemmican, bread, jam, and erbswurst soup as well as some cocoa. At about six-thirty we began to go to bed and about seven we finished this frigid process! The "beds" weren't so bad; pine boughs, an empty sleeping bag, then a bag with me in it, then another bag, and finally all my clothes on top. This last "coverlet" didn't amount to much as I wore most of my clothes.

I kept my head in the open air only about half of the night, being afraid that I might freeze my ears and nose!

When the next morning at last came the temperature was seventeen degrees below Zero! The snow lay in a fine powder over everything. It had been blown in by the wind during the night.

I summoned up my greatest nerve and leaped from my bag just after Kelly had led me a good example. Our boots were frozen tight. We ought to have slept with them, but had forgotten about them completely.

Several attempts to start a fire in the forty-mile-an-hour wind proved futile. Nothing would keep the wood burning. And, even worse, it was so cold that we couldn't take off our gloves to get out our food. Our fingers would get numb with cold in a few seconds.

I think that we might have stayed and sacrificed breakfast had it been a good day, but the weather was poor and the movie camera wouldn't work in the cold, so we banged our shoes into shape with an axe, jammed them on, and ran for the Pinkham Notch camp where we knew that Joe Dodge, its keeper, could get us a little warm food.

CHAPTER IV

PREPARATION

Preparations are always the most terrific job. Usually it is harder to prepare for a trip than to make it. But there is a certain joy that I get out of preparing. I always feel that the trip is so near at hand I get really quite excited. Lists must be made and train reservations and ticket got, and when you get to the stage of greasing up your boots you are nearly frantic with the desire to get out and climb with them.

These were the feelings that rushed through us all last term up at school. I must have made a new clean list every day, nervously tearing the old one into a thousand little pieces. "For Mother to get"; "be sure to get this before you go"; these were the titles of a couple of my sacred documents. Sometimes, against all rules and in face of dire penalties, I would sneak from my bed to my study and scratch down "can opener," "shoe grease," or the like to be sure that I would not forget them and remain uncomfortable for the whole trip.

At last the final day came. School was over and I spent the whole morning ransacking Boston for lens shades and fittings for my camera and a thousand other things that I had scratched on my little (now tremendous) list.

The list was finally completed and I returned home laden low with my purchases. The whole afternoon was used up by packing.

Tappey Turner, my friend, and I were going to use no suitcases or trunks at all. All of our food, clothes, and equipment was to be carried on our backs, and we were to go to the mountains in hiking clothes to avoid all the extra bother of wearing city clothes and getting rid of them when we got there.

Our work was all finished in the afternoon and at midnight we took the train for Portland, Maine. The next morning at six o'clock we went through the usual mess and mix-up of changing railroads and at 7:20 we left for Gorham, New Hampshire, on the Grand Trunk Line. Three hours more on the train brought us to our destination.

At Gorham my good friend Mr. Bickford met us and told us that three days before four packers had taken a load of our food up Mount Washington and left it in the little hut on top. That news took a load off my mind.

All of our previous trips had been made in vacations as was this one. I had been up Mount Washington five times before, four times at Christmas and one at Easter. The two ascents that we made last Christmas, as I have told, were both ended by a night or two spent in the little hut on top of the mountain. This Easter we planned to go up the mountain and spend a week on top, making the hut our base and climbing around on the other peaks.

This long stay made a lot of food necessary, so we had hired our men from Gorham to pack up what they could, leaving the rest for us to take when we came. My fears had been greatly raised about our packers just three days before we arrived, owing to the very bad weather that had been prevailing in the mountains.

We packed all of our equipment onto an automobile and started off for the famous Glen House, eight miles from Gorham.

At Boston there had been no snow at all, neither had there been any at Portland, but here at Gorham there was well over a foot of new powdery snow. Besides, the sky was gray and it looked just as if it were getting ready to start snowing again.

Luckily the auto-road to the Glen House had been traveled over recently when the car had brought in our packers three days before, so we had no trouble at all in getting through. Just before the Glen the auto struck some deep drifts which took some tough bucking and shoveling before we could get through them. Then the trouble came. Only fifty yards from the little hotel part of our rear axle smashed in two! The chauffeur tried to explain to me how it happened and why it broke, but it is still a mystery to me. At any rate it was lucky that it happened where it did and not far-ther off down the road.

In summer the Glen is a crowded, noisy resort for the tourists who swarm up Mount Washington in autos along the well-known "Carriage Road." At Easter time the little hotel is entirely deserted save for its two keepers, Mr. and Mrs. Pike, who stay there all the year 'round. The winds howl about the house and barn and the drifts of fine snow pile up deep about it.

So it was when we came there, there were over two feet of snow on the level and we stumbled across the drifted lawn to the porch from the disabled auto with our packs and skis. Mr. Pike had met us a little down the road with a shovel to help us through the drifts and had greeted me with his usual cheery, "How are you, boy?" Now it was Mrs. Pike's turn, and she shook our hands cor-dially as we struggled up to the porch and deposited our loads. Yes, she remembered Tappey very well.

She especially recalled the terrific games of "pitch" that had been waged in the kitchen just two years before between Mr. Pike and me on one side and Ray Evans, our guide, and Tappey on the other. It hurts me deeply to relate that the second combination was usually victorious! Nevertheless, Mr. Pike and I were all set for a terrible comeback. We were quite sure that we would beat Mrs. Pike and Tappey off the face of the earth that evening at a game of cards.

The road to the south of the Glen (Gorham lies to the north) leads to Jackson Village, fifteen miles away. The "height of land" or highest point between the Glen and Jackson is called the Pinkham Notch. The Appalachian Mountain Club keeps a hut there for climbers, open summer and winter, under the manage-ment of Joe Dodge. Joe, as we all call him, has been in the employment of the A.M.C. for a number of years and just recently they have made him manager of all the club's huts on the Mount Washington range.

The Crampons and One of the Shoes Worn by the Author.

He and his wife and Ross Hinter were keeping the Camp this winter and when Mr. Putnam and I went home in January after the Christmas climbing we left a lot of our stuff at Pinkham (the familiar name for the hut). So after lunch Tappey and I put on our skis and left the Glen to ski on to Pinkham (three miles) for this equipment, which consisted of some rope, ice-creepers, ice-axes, and cooking utensils.

All went well. We found all the stuff and were back at the Glen in time for a six o'clock supper. Then after supper, before the "pitch" battle was scheduled, Mr. Pike and I dumped our packs and made them up again all pretty nearly equal in weight except for one which weighed ten pound more than the rest. This was for a packman from Gorham, Ross by name, who was to come up the next morning by auto with Don Brown of New York, the third member of the party. We planned to have Ross take as much as he could up to the top because without that help our packs would have been too heavy. As it was they amounted to forty-five pounds each except for Ross's which weighed fifty-five.

When the canvas sacks had been filled up Mr. Pike and I bound them onto "pack-boards." These are made of two parallel strips of wood about eighteen inches long and four inches wide, placed two inches apart and fastened together with little staves. This rig is fixed onto your back by two straps like any other pack. Each pack-board is equipped with a twenty-foot coil of clothesline, and you bind onto the two boards anything that you want to carry. The boards fit your back *very* comfortably and in this way you can carry lots of queer-shaped pointed articles, which would be very uncomfortable sticking into your back through an ordinary rucksack.

This job completed Mr. Pike and I had a fight talk and then issued into the kitchen to the fray. Tappey and Mrs. Pike had prepared the cards and table and we began the most spirited game of pitch that I have ever played. I would describe the game if I could, but it is the only game that I know except Rum and I have practically forgotten that, so I'm sure that I should have a hard time!

Failure is always crowned by success *if you persist*. The fight talk had its effects and Mr. Pike and I came through to a sweeping victory, and after telegraphing the family that we were all safe at the Glen we went to bed in high spirits—at least Mr. Pike and I did!

CHAPTER V

ON TO THE HALFWAY HOUSE

The next morning we weren't awakened in the novel French style at midnight or one o'clock. Mrs. Pike clanged a big dinner-bell at six o'clock. Not one of us woke up. Mr. Pike came upstairs in about ten minutes and battered in our doors each in turn.

It was a terrible day. The clouds hung low over the mountains and the temperature was way up to thirty-five degrees. Water could be heard dripping from the roof. However, no matter what the weather was, we had to get all of our provisions up to the Halfway House by that night if not to the top. Who could tell? Maybe the weather would clear off by noon.

A good bacon-and-egg breakfast, helped along by some famous Pike cornbread and marmalade, put us on our feet. By seven o'clock we were all on the porch, ready to start, watching the clouds as they rolled back and forth over the "range." If my Chamonix guide had been there he would surely have said, "Pas beau temps aujourd'hui, Brad" ("We'll have no good weather today, Brad").

We were obviously in for a bad day of it. All of our skis had been waxed the night before with special Norwegian wax so that they would slip fast over soft, powdery snow. What good would they be today? Perhaps the snow would get a little powdery and

less slushy as we climbed upwards. At any rate skis would be better in wet snow than snowshoes.

We set out across the field in front of the Glen House, stamping and kicking to try to get our skis to slide. All these attempts
proved useless, so we made the best of a terrible day and hurried
along walking on skis instead of sliding.

The first half mile from the Glen leads you downhill and across
a river to a meadow. Then the road up Mount Washington begins,
winding in a series of long, lazy zigzags all over the slopes in order
to make it less steep. The wet snow caked so deeply on the bottoms of our skis that it doubled and sometimes even tripled their
weight. Once I stopped to try walking without the skis at all.

One try was enough! I sunk in up to my hips with my skiless leg
and had a hard time hauling myself back to the surface again.
Every hundred and fifty feet we stopped and kicked the snow off
our skis. Then we rested about a minute or two and were off again
up the long, steady, easy grade.

A grade like the Carriage Road is very hard on one's muscles;
much harder, in fact, than a varied grade—one that is sometimes
steep and sometimes easy. Our legs began to hurt terribly after we
had made the first mile (there are four of them to the Halfway
House).

Every step we took our packs seemed to get heavier and heavier. It's all right to have your pack get heavier when it begins at
twenty or even thirty pounds, but when it begins at fifty pounds—
well, there is a limit to everything!

If it had been a beautiful day, the marvelous views that you get
from the road would have taken our attention off ourselves a little. But the weather got worse and worse. At a bend just above the
one-mile mark it rained a little. Then it began to snow, then it
sleeted and finally stopped doing everything and just stayed warm,
nasty, and cloudy.

At the two-mile post my skis were about fifty times their ordinary weight, I'm willing to wager, and my pack had increased to
at least a hundred and fifty pounds. The going got simply awful. It
had snowed there a few days before and the road was a long series
of drifts, some of them as much as ten or fifteen feet deep.

Up one drift, down it, up another, down that, stop and scrape your skis, rest a minute. Up one drift, down it, up another, down that, stop again. That was the routine for the next mile! The snow was now falling in big, wet flakes which melted the moment that they touched anything. Our shirts were off and this continual mid-March shower cooled us off very soothingly.

At a point about two and a half miles from the Glen, Tappey and I decided that two-minute rests weren't enough for us. So we took off each other's packs and sat down upon the railing of an old bridge which stuck up a foot or so through the snow. The longer we sat the more tired our legs got, and after about fifteen minutes we got up and prepared to get under way again.

I was helping Tappey get his pack on when all of a sudden his ski slipped. He had had both arms through the straps and was just straightening up when it happened, so the weight of the pack dragged him about two feet down into the slushy snow. I laughed so hard at seeing him in this hopeless fix that I fell over myself. If I had not landed near a little tree we would have both been in a terrible mess. As it was I managed to shin up the tree enough to get my skis under me again. Then I helped snorting, puffing Tappey to his feet and after we had wiped the hunks of wet snow from ourselves we started off again.

In the forty minutes that we had wasted playing around like babies in the drifts Ross and Don had been going ahead, thinking that we were following only a short distance behind. As for us, we didn't know where we should find them and didn't much care. We would all be too tired to go on to the top that day, so we hoped that we should meet them at the Halfway House.

Our rest had done us no good. We marched upwards in short spurts, panting for breath after every few feet, yet determined to get to the house before noon. At eleven forty-five we passed the three mile post: four hours and forty minutes from the Glen. We had made the last mile, including the rest of forty minutes, in an hour and three-quarters. (A friend and I had climbed the whole mountain without packs a year ago last Christmas in four hours!)

At the three and one-half mile mark we met Don and Ross ski-ing gaily downwards. When they saw us they stopped and said

Rounding the "Horn."

they were going to the Glen for the night and would come up again the next day. They had had enough of climbing for one day. The weather was very bad above the treeline (the Halfway point) and it would be impossible to go on to the top anyway.

We urged them to stay the night at the Halfway House, but we might as well have talked to two doorposts. In five minutes they were gone and we were plodding on again in the same old dreary way. They had taken only ten minutes from the house on skis, so we hurried on (at the rate of nearly a mile an hour) and soon the yellow structure appeared beyond a curve ahead.

As we came around the corner a gust if icy wind struck us. The mountain was beginning to turn into itself again. It might be a good day the next day. Blast upon blast of frigid air, laden with powdery, cutting particles of snow, struck us as we forged ahead towards the house, now only a few hundred feet away. This added torture, when we were so nearly dead from exhaustion anyway, made us desperate. We fought foot by foot, balancing and leaning against the wind until at last we came into the shelter of the house and threw ourselves on the ground.

A moment was enough to let us get our breath. Then each of us helped the other with his pack. We took off our skis and scraped the caked snow from them so that it wouldn't freeze during the night. Don could go down if he wanted to. We were out for a little adventure and were all too glad at a chance like this. Our skis scraped, we stood them up against a sheltered wall of the house. Then we mounted the steps and opened the door. It was almost pitch dark inside.

The appearance of the house in broad daylight with its gloomy boarded-up windows and nasty yellow paint is bad enough. The appearance of that room as I forced the door open, and as the wind whistled by eddying in a load of biting snow particles, was enough to give one a nightmare! Tappey pushed me in and slammed the door behind us.

CHAPTER VI

THE HALFWAY HOUSE

I stumbled into the empty room and threw my pack into a corner. Tappey followed my example and then we began to forage for everything. First: where were the packs that Don and Ross had left? Since they had all the food in them they were extremely important, and we must get everything that we were going to use out of the packs before darkness fell or we should find ourselves in a bad fix.

A very short search revealed the packs on a table in the front room. The room was bare like all the rest, but the boards had fallen off one of the windows so we could see quite plainly what was around us.

A little pile of snow had accumulated upon the floor where part of a pane of glass was broken out. The table was strewn with rope, crampons, ice-axes, and food. The house was as cold as a very chilly icebox and we moved around quickly in our tour of inspection. The little plan which appears on the opposite page will give a good idea of the arrangement of the rooms in the house. From the front room we went on through a low doorway into a room on the exposed side of the house.

This, too, was pitch dark and fearfully cold. There was a small stove in the middle of the floor with a few frost-covered pieces of kindling in front of it. Another little hole of a room appeared

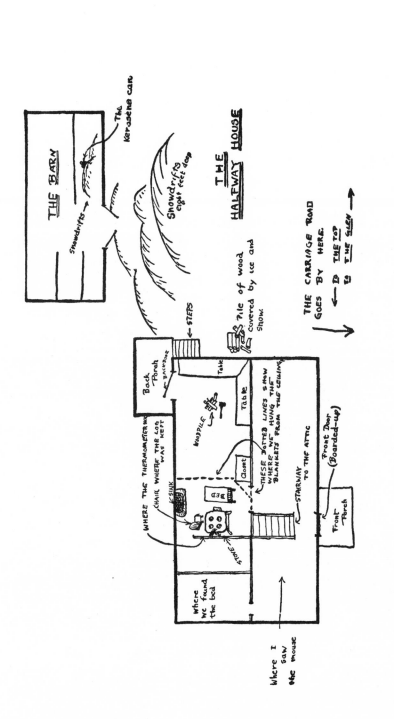

before us, but it was so dark that I had to dig the flashlight from my pack so as to be able to see anything. Two very damp mattresses lay on the floor and a thoroughly rusted bedstead leaned against the wall. Above this was a line of hooks upon which hung three or four wet, nasty old coats left there by carriage-road workmen in the fall. A steep, short flight of stairs led us to the attic where there was a huge pile of mattresses all too wet to use.

The search only took us a few minutes and we descended from the attic stairs on the run to save time in our wood-chopping operations. An old yellow shed lies behind the house and this was our next objective. The door was jammed shut by a huge snowdrift, but we managed to trample around enough to make a path through to the shed and then our combined efforts opened the door.

A thin film of snow lay over everything and with some difficulty we found a hammer, some nails, and an old axe. Tappey brought these back to the main house and left me to do some more exploring. I knocked to pieces a couple of boxes and a sawhorse and piled them by the door to be transported for kindling wood. Then I espied an old can, way off in a corner, sticking its nozzle out of a snowdrift.

Maybe it was kerosene! I waded through the drift. Sure enough! Something splashed in it. I hauled my prey out onto the open floor and was just opening the nozzle as Tappey came in. What luck we were having. A moment later a drifted shelf revealed a lantern without a wick in it. And as Tappey was bringing this to the center of the room I discovered that our can had nearly two gallons of kerosene in it. A wick which I had put into my leather jacket pocket at Christmas filled the bill, and we stepped out into the roaring wind, bolted the door again and made a dash for the Halfway House.

We didn't know the time, as we had forgotten a watch and the clock (not going) was in the bottom of my knapsack. But since the house was getting a little under the shadow of the mountain we thought that it was about three o'clock. Besides, we had met Ross and Don about three hours before. We got the clock out and set it, for fun, at three minutes pass three. Then we set to work again. The room which we had first entered had a big stove in it, so we decided to make that part of the house our sleeping quarters. There was no door between it and the room in which the packs were and it itself was too big to heat all night with the single stove and the limited supply of wood. So we took the five blankets that were in our packs and nailed two over the door. Two others we hung on a string across the big room, cutting its size about in half. The fifth blanket we laid on one of the beds which we had dragged in from the little room and placed before the stove.

All this completed, we began to cut wood like mad. Benches, tables, boxes, and logs from a frozen pile outside served us for quite a heap of firewood. Tappey cut this as I prepared the stove for action by cleaning it out and laying inside an extra scientifically built pile of slivers, chips, kindling, and logs. Another pile of wood covered with ice and snow was put in the oven of the stove and then the fire was started.

An utter failure at first, my pile was helped along by a dose of kerosene of which we had plenty. This time it blazed away finely and soon we had a merry fire going. As the wood in the oven dried out we transferred it also to a pile behind the stove. We also placed behind the stove a tremendous thermometer nearly four feet high, advertising Glenwood Ranges.

In about an hour the house began to get warm enough so that we could take off a few of our outside clothes and loosen up our boots. Ice melting from underneath the stove caused a tremendous puddle all around the bed, and just where we wanted to stand while cooking. An old broom was continually in use brushing the dirty black water across the room and under a table where it leaked through the floor and was out of the way!

Supper wasn't long in the cooking. I was "Chief Chef" and prepared one of the most delicious meals that I have ever "made" consisting of canned baked beans, canned spaghetti, and cocoa—the best dishes that I know for a climbing meal. Cans may be heavy to carry and canned food may not be real "backwoods camping," but after all what one wants is *real nourishing* food and, besides, a can of food takes up about half as much room as its equivalent in uncanned goods.

Well, as I said, the supper went to the right spot. The clock read just seven o'clock when we started to eat, and when the dishes were cleaned in boiling water made from melted snow, we swept the pools of water from the floor. Then we made a sort of footrest out of a small plank with which to keep our feet dry, and started a game of pitch with two "dummy" hands.

We were still rather heavily dressed, and it would have been an amusing sight to see us leaning over the table (and old board found in a nearby room, balanced on our knees) playing pitch by the light of one, faint lantern. I sat beside the door on the stove and occasionally shoved a log in to keep the temperature above freezing. Since Tappey and I each played two hands, the game became rather complicated.

Two games of this with an intermission for woodchopping between them brought the time to 9:30. Then we started another chopping campaign, for we wanted to have as much sleep as we could during the next few hours. By ten o'clock we had a fine heap of wood, both drying in the oven and piled up under the stove.

Together we managed to drag in one of the damp mattresses from the other room. This was laid on the bed, then I got some old sacks and a sweater for a pillow. We could spare no blankets for sleeping purposes as they were all *very* necessary to keep the warm air from circulating around the room and leaving our little comfortable corner.

The plan for the night was formed during supper and the agreements were as follows: The night was to be divided into four two-hour watches. Tappey was to take the first one, and then we were to alternate, the man on watch stoking the fire, sweeping the water off into the corner, and seeing that the outer door stayed shut—the wind had blown it open twice already with its violent gusts. The watcher also was to keep "the log," a record of everything that happened during the hours of his watches.

Just before I went to bed I went outside to get two buckets of snow to leave on the fire for making cocoa for breakfast and for boiling a couple of the dozen eggs that we had lugged up (we didn't yet know whether they had survived the rigorous ascent of the morning!).

The wind was something stupendous, sweeping, lashing, tearing the snow from the soft drifts which covered the mountain. It whipped them through the air at a mad rate. Every particle of the frozen clouds that touched my face in the few seconds that I was out on my two short trips for snow nearly cut my face in two. What a night!

The clouds were all around us in a heavy, thick covering, matting the trees and all the objects outside with a white film of frost. The temperature outside the door registered twelve degrees above Zero on the little thermometer that we had placed there, lashed to a nail.

I slammed the door behind me and a gust of wind blew it back in my face with a bang and a scream. I called Tappey over and together we succeeded in barricading it with a heavy log. Then we returned to our little den and I was asleep in a jiffy, all muffled up in my fur-lined hood, leather jacket, and sweater.

CHAPTER VII

A WILD NIGHT

"The Log"
The Halfway House—Mount Washington

Thursday, March 22, 1928
(E.T.T. Recording)

10:07 P.M. —Assumed first office as watchman and guardian of the
peace.

10:12 —Brad tossing about fitfully. A gust of wind just made
him shriek in a weird manner. Going to read.

11:00 —Temperature up to sixty-eight degrees now. Burned
my finger opening stove.

11:11 —Sixty-nine degrees.

11:11 —Got so excited over temperature that I dropped my
handkerchief on the wet floor and stepped on it.

11:30 —Deeply engrossed in *The Canary Murder Case* when
he (Brad, not the canary) gave an alarming grunt.
Brewed myself two cups of hot cocoa and ate a couple of marshmallows.

Watch II
(B.W. Recording)

12:03 A.M.—Friday, March 23—"Official Duty" begins. Tappey
has settled down at last after many violent outbursts
of coughing. His cold seems worse. He looks very
comfortable, but (from experience!) I know all too
well that he isn't. He has discovered the mouldy
coats of two workmen in the other room and after
careful drying and occasional sniffing he has covered
himself with these dainty articles, as well as his
sweater, Don Brown's sweater, and a parka (fur-lined
combination hood and coat made of airplane cloth).

12:09^1/$_2$ —Temperature sixty-three degrees. Getting colder fast.
Wind going down a little outside.

12:19   —Temperature outside is at fourteen degrees. Fog and
snow with a tough breeze, gusts exceeding thirty-five
miles an hour. Out only a moment to look at thermometer and returned wet from head to foot by frost
particles. My feet are particularly damp. I have
placed another board under them as the floor is a
veritable swimming pool from a cake of ice melting
under the stove. We haven't yet been able to pry out
the ice; it seems stuck tight to the floor.

12:29   —Back door blown open by a terrific gust of wind. The
crash gave me an awful scare. Soaked my feet closing
and barricading it again. The wind is increasing and
the chimney is drawing very badly—clouds of smoke
are pouring into the room.

12:32   —Tappey is sleeping soundly but not sound*less*ly.

12:42   —Tappey snoring violently—wood running low.

12:51   —Wind increasing rapidly—Temperature 59^3/$_4$ degrees.
Chimney is drawing very badly. I can see my breath
less than six inches from the stove.

1:04   —Temperature has dropped to fifty-eight degrees.
House is really chilly. Am going to re-stoke and blow
on fire.

The Author on One of the Snow Slopes.

1:11   —Fifty-seven degrees. Fire going full blast, but it is cold less than a foot from the stove.

1:33½   —My work has been rewarded. Temperature now fifty-eight degrees. But it's still very cold. The wind is blowing like fury and something upstairs is crashing at every gust. Tappey just came to for a moment, but is again wrapped in slumber. As I quote these temperatures it must be remembered that the thermometer is 2½ feet from the back of the stove (red hot) and less than a foot from the stove pipe which is nearly red hot.

1:45   —Tappey jumped from the bed with a yell owing to lack of warmth and comfort. He is now at the other end of the room inspecting the fuel supply (very low!). He has just dropped Don's sweater in the muck on the floor.

2:00   —Thermometer reads sixty degrees now. With our combined efforts the fire is raging despite the blasted old wind. Tappey is chopping wood in the far corner of the room. I nearly stepped on a tiny mouse while I was getting the last few bits of kindling from the other room.

Third Watch
(E.T.T. cuts wood, B.W. recording)

2:05   —Thermometer outside ten degrees—inside sixty-one degrees. Tappey's efforts are being crowned with success. He is a wizard with a fire! He has just remarked that the ashes in the grate will look like a junk-heap owing to our demolition of everything demolishable *and then some* for fuel. (The words in italics were added to "The Log" by E.T.T. during the next half hour while B.W. was asleep.)

(Here B.W. goes to bed, E.T.T. begins recording.)

2:10   —Have donned some extra clothing—getting hungry. Wind blowing fiercely—feel it my duty to admit that

Tappey Turner has done a yeoman's task in supplying kindling for the fire. Just the same, may have to wake Brad to split some heavy stuff. I have grave fears for the fire, which is *"not so hot."* Suffering from a couple of deep cuts made by nails in the kindling.

(Here "The Log" dropped on the floor—the original copy is yellow for half a page on account of its landing in the muck.)

3:04   —My coughing seems just about to break even with the wind. The first tends to blow the walls out, the second to drive them in—result: the walls are sometimes practically perpendicular.

3:24   —After sundry preliminaries such as dropping the cards severally into the muck on the floor, I played six holes of golf (a kind of solitaire), the stroke, being 1, 2, 3, 4, 5, and 7—most unusual.

4:04   —Have yelled no less than three times at an unresponsive Brad to get him to relieve me and write the epilog. Maybe he has frozen to death—In this event I may have enough breakfast!

Fourth (Last) Watch
(B.W. Recording)

4:05   —I have just come on duty after much pushing and yelling from Tappey who finally let loose an alarm clock right in my ear. This woke me up and I got up to find the temperature fifty-five degrees—the coldest yet since about four o'clock yesterday afternoon. It must be mighty cold outside, but I don't dare look at the thermometer for fear of soaking my feet on the floor (I am still resting my feet on the boards mentioned sometime back).

4:15   —The wind is blowing like fury and since I am not sneezing *à la Turner*, the house is rising, shaking, banging, and falling like a ship in a storm. The fire is grand and using very little wood. (It hasn't been stoked for forty-five minutes.)

4:51 —Dawn is beginning to creep in upon the camp of the dar-
      ing adventurers! Very faint daylight is filtering through
      the fog outside and the heavily frosted windows. Fire
      going like a breeze. The whole house just shook with a
      blast of wind. Thermometer 53 degrees. I have now got
      on both my leather jacket and parka and am still cold.

5:00 —Tappey is sleeping soundly and the bed with him on
      it looks very much like one of the supply bins of the
      second-hand athletic clothing store at school. There
      is no possible clue from one end of the mass of
      clothes to the other to prove that there is *nothing but
      clothes* there, save an occasional snort or puff. It is
      slowly getting lighter now.

5:06 —Temperature—fifty-one degrees!

6:02 —Temperature forty-four degrees! Just got up and
      looked out the door. Without any exaggeration the
      wind is blowing seventy miles an hour. (Tappey
      agrees to this, too.) It is blowing like last summer on
      Mont Blanc—there is not a cloud in the sky either.
      The snow is rushing about like nothing human,
      sucking around "the Horn" (the four mile curve of
      the carriage road about two hundred yards above the
      Halfway House) like a great whirlpool.

6:34 —Despite all our efforts the door has smashed over a
      huge block of hardwood and is open again!

6:55 —Breakfast ready, prepared by B.W. consisting of two
      soft-boiled eggs each, and some cocoa. The house is a
      little warmer now, but I cannot tell the temperature
      because the indoor thermometer is outside to take the
      place of the small one broken by the wind last night.

7:30 —Outside thermometer ten degrees in the shade.
      Glorious day—wind slightly decreased in intensity.

9:16 —We just found out from Don (two hours from the
      Glen on snowshoes, arriving at 8:40) that his watch
      set at the Glen read 9:15. Last night, as I mentioned,
      Tappey and I set our clock by a guess and hit the time
      within one minute!

A TERRIFIC HAUL

"The Log," Continued
Camden Cottage—Summit of Mount Washington

Friday, March 23, 1928
(B.W. recording)

At ten-thirty we left for the summit after having sorted out our stuff. Ross could not come up to help us on account of symptoms of appendicitis (he left early from the Glen to go to Gorham). We left everything that was luxurious on the table in the Halfway House and stuck the skis in a snowdrift on the lee side of the house. Then we strapped on our crampons and set out up the road around the Horn.

We took a couple of pictures of Mts. Jefferson and Adams (see map) in a warm sunny spot. Then as we rounded the Horn curve it got icy cold. As is the usual case, just above the Horn a succession of patches of glare ice and deep drifts of snow slowed us up and tired us considerably under the weight of our forty-five-pound packs of provisions. The wind began to pipe up at the four-and-one-quarter-mile mark and was hitting a good forty miles an hour. A quarter mile of drift-plunging brought us to the spot where the old telephone line from the Halfway House to the summit of Mount Washington crossed the road. There we left the road on

Tappey a Hundred Yards Below the Wind-Swept Summit of Mount Washington.

our left and followed the line of low, ancient telephone posts directly up the steep grade, thus avoiding a wide swing that the road makes between the fifth- and sixth-mile mark. The day was cloudless and glorious, but the wind, blowing with it a huge load of frost particles and loose snow, seemed to cut our faces in two. We had on our windproof furry parkas, sweaters under them, and heavy gloves, so that our bodies were all right, but the important problem was how to keep our faces from being ripped to pieces.

The wind where we were was only about forty miles an hour, but up ahead of us on the crest of the ridge we could see a terrific gale blowing the snow along before it. It was a magnificent sight—the white clouds of snow racing at stupendous speed, out-lines in sharp contrast against the gorgeous blue of the sky.

Steep slopes of snow intervened between us and the upper bend of the road for which we were heading. The struggle up the grade was pretty bad. The wind buffeted us harder and harder every step we took. It came in sharp sudden gusts, loosening our foothold and balance. The worst part of this fight upwards was the gusts of wind. We would lean our whole weight against one of these to keep from blowing over, then the wind would stop altogether for a second, making us stagger about ten feet to the right as we tried to regain our balance. This staggering was absolutely unavoidable and *terribly* tiring.

Just before we reached the road again Don left Tappey and me and hurried ahead as fast as he was able on account of his feet which were getting very cold. Tappey and I decided to take it easily, as we had the whole day ahead of us and we didn't want to hurry a bit. We battled on together with the soft drifts and fierce wind till we reached the road once more, some forty-five minutes after having left it below. The cut-off gained about a half mile for us. Just as we reached the road Don disappeared for good around a curve a short distance ahead. Tappey and I took a very small number of rests and kept plugging most of the time so as not to let our feet get cold. A ten minute sit-down in that wind and temperature would mean two frozen feet without question.

Plug! Plug! Plug! Another half hour brought us to the edge of the "cow pasture," a wide, sloping expanse around which the road makes a horseshoe curve. Years ago they tried to keep some cows there for milk for people in the summit house in summer. Here another cut-off gained us a quarter mile and placed us on the road again a few hundred yards above the seven-mile mark. Only three-quarters of a mile left to go!

Now the worst part of the struggle commenced. The wind had increased in violence to at least sixty miles an hour and threatened to blow us over at every stop. We could see the gusts as they came sweeping up the slope towards us with their white whirl of snow and could usually prepare ourselves for each one before it arrived. The packs on our back served as sails and continually spoiled our balance.

At last! A bend at the seven-and-one-half-mile point brought us into sight of the summit. It seemed to me like a magic citadel, its tiny cluster of buildings soaring up ahead of us, hidden now and then in the furious blasts of white, smoky snow, lashed and hurled over it by the wind.

The road now became flat and swung a little to the left, bringing our backs to the wind. And with our packs still serving us as sails we raced across this level spot to the base of the cone of the peak.

Tappey and I were walking about six feet apart during the most intense part of a wild gust of wind. All of a sudden a dead calm came. We both staggered as usual. Then another gust struck us both unprepared and we ran into each other with a crash! We both sat down, rolling over and over on the ice which covered the road.

Another struggle put us on our feet again and a minute later, after we had progressed some fifty feet (it was very slow work!) a heavy gust swept my pack off my back and it fell into the road. It had been loosened by my fall. Both Tappey and I looked at it in despair. We were both so tired that we couldn't fix it onto the pack-board again. The board was still on my back with its rope blowing out like a four-foot streamer.

As we watched, the pack blew across the road (it weighed forty-five pounds, remember) and struck against the wall at the edge. We were now but three hundred yards from the top, so we decided to leave the pack where it was in its firmly wedged position and hurry on the short distance to the hut on the summit.

I felt as if every gust would blow me away with my weight decreased from 200 pounds to only 150! And I found myself dancing along ahead of poor, weary Tappey as if I had just started a moment before! It was marvelous what a difference of forty-five pounds could make. A hundred and fifty feet more walking brought us into the lee of the summit mound and in ten minutes we were both entering the door of Camden Cottage, the little hut on the summit. The climb was over.

The excitement, however, was far from being at an end. When I burst open the door and strode in, stamping my boots to knock off the snow from them, I saw Don sitting on a bench near the little stove gazing at the ceiling. I guessed that he had started the fire, and gave him a rousing, "Hello, fellow, we did it!" A grunt was my only answer. His eyes remained perfectly blank as he gazed at us.

Something must be wrong. I tossed my pack-board onto the cot in the corner and opened the stove. Tappey flung himself exhausted upon the bench beside Don, who appeared paralyzed. Not a thing was in the stove except two, big, wet logs!

CHAPTER IX

IN CAMDEN

Far back in the tiny stove an old bit of damp newspaper was smoldering. I snatched out the logs and paper and leveled off the ashes. In the meantime, Tappey had cast off his pack and was looking about on the shelves for some tea. While he was doing this I took out my knife and slivered up some very thin kindling. This, doused with kerosene from a can in the corner, started up a rousing blaze. I added a few hunks of larger kindling and then a log. Then we both ran out to a drift piled up against the Tip-Top House and each got a large bowl-full of snow.

When we got back into the hut we put these on the stove to melt. Five minutes later we had a cup of warm tea for Don and in ten minutes a cup of steaming, boiling tea was coursing down his throat. It was wonderful to see the change in him. His teeth stopped chattering and he began to be sensible again!

Three small boxes of Sunmaid raisins next fell our prey and then a number of bars of chocolate. When we were all thoroughly warmed out I decided that it was just about time to go down to get my pack. When I said this to Tappey, Don startled us both saying this his pack had shared the same fate as mine. Continued falls on the rocks just below the summit had dumped it some three hundred yards from the cabin.

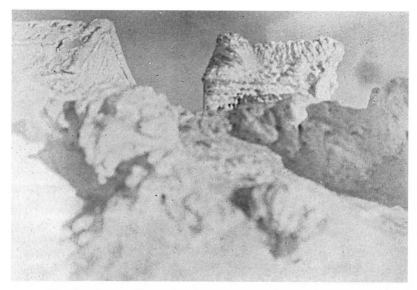

Camden Cottage (Center) with the Summit House (Left corner).

We all started out at once. Tappey having made a compact with me that if I would sit down in the midst of all the wind and securely tie my pack onto the pack-board he would take it up to the hut for me. This seemed exceptionally good to me! In fact it was too good an offer to reject.

We both raced down the road in an attempt to keep the warmth in us that we had just gained in the hut. Don disappeared over a little ledge to our left and began the search for his pack. I soon discovered that I had got all of a good job tying up my pack. Gust after gust of howling, screaming wind laden with snow lashed at me. I braced myself against the wall at the edge of the road and worked slowly, but surely, undoing tangles and tying up knots tightly. Tappey watched me from behind a sheltered rock roaring with laughter.

At last I signaled to him that it was his turn to act. I ran to him with the pack, clapped it on his back and then made for a bend in the road with him at top speed. My chilled fingers began to regain their warmth and Tappey's face once more broke into a smile as we rounded this curve and stopped in the shelter of a little barn just below the summit. (It was there that they used to keep the horses when they climbed the mountain in the old days and they keep the cars there now.)

A moment of rest and we were off again. Halfway from the barn to the top I pointed out Mount Monadnock to Tappey as it loomed up on the horizon. It was cut cold and clear against the gorgeous blue sky as we saw it between the whirls of flying snow that swept by us.

When we got back to the hut three minutes later we found Don just entering the door. No sooner had we laid down our packs on the cot than a loud rap sounded. The door burst open and two men slipped through the narrow opening. They were covered with white frost from head to foot and had no packs. They had come up from the Glen and were planning to go down again that afternoon.

It didn't take us long to induce them to spend the night with us and, as a matter of fact, it was really pretty late to start down anyway. We had arrived on top at 3:05 and it was now half past three or quarter to four. Don, mostly recovered, and I left the hut hotfoot to get some pictures of it and the other buildings deeply covered with their mantle of frost-feathers, ice, and snow.

Four pictures proved enough for us! The wind was so nasty that we had to brace the camera against rocks to get a twenty-fifth-of-a-second exposure without blurring the film. When we returned to Camden Cottage, Tappey, who thought himself lucky not to be a photographer, introduced us to the newcomers, Paul Bartlett and Dave Inglis of Amherst. A half-hour of very strenuous labor straightened out the hut from a Babel of disorder to the cleanest, shipshape little shack in New England. Our packs were dumped into the cot and two hammocks hung up from the beams above our heads. Then the can-opener began to work and Don heated the stove until the pipe turned red. A savory mess of tomato and vegetable soup (mixed), corned beef hash, and instant cocoa made us feel like different people.

A big can of hash disappeared in a couple of minutes and cocoa went down by the gallon. After supper the dishwashing crew (myself and Don) cleaned up the kitchen part of the mess, while Paul, Dave, and Tappey split wood for the night. A pile of big wood in one corner speedily diminished and turned into a larger pile of wonderful, dry kindling and medium-sized logs next to the stove.

By the time that our supper was done, the dishes washed, and the wood cut we all began to feel like going to "bed." It was only about eight o'clock, but we had had a hard day and we all turned in after leaving three kettles of snow on the stove to use for making cereal and cocoa for breakfast.

Don and I took the hammocks, Tappey drew the bed, and Dave and Paul insisted on sleeping (we don't yet know whether either of them slept at all) sandwiched in on a wide bench below my hammock. They said that they would take turns at stoking the fire, and were certainly mighty nice to take the job, as Tappey and I were all ready for a little sleep after our night at the Halfway House.

TWO NIGHTS ON TOP

Crash! I woke up with a start and saw Tappey sitting up in bed by the light that flickered through the chinks in the stove. Crash! Another roar came and the whole cabin shook. Then all was still. My hammock was swinging wildly back and forth because I was sitting up in it, and I lay down again in a hurry before it could pitch me out onto the stove.

We were all awake. Don's watch said that it was two o'clock in the morning. The fire kept on flickering and it was still once more save for the whistling and howling of the wind and the creaking of the hut as it was strained by the wintry blasts. We all fell asleep and before we knew it, it was six in the morning.

Gray daylight came in through the windows and lit up the whole room. I leaped to the floor and shuffled outside in my moccasins to see what had caused the two great crashes at two o'clock.

Of all the tragedies that ever took place this was the worst. I opened the door and walked out in my shirtsleeves. The thermometer outside registered forty degrees! It was really warm! After a few steps I saw the cause of the midnight crashes. Every bit of frost had been ripped off the building by the wind, and two great loads of this heavy icy material had hit our cabin as it was

The Author Developing Pictures in the Attic of Camden Cottage.

blown by. Hardly a frost-feather remained on our own hut. Camden was as bleak and gray as in summer.

I went back inside and told the half-awake remainder of the party the bad news. No good pictures could be taken that day. However, the sight of the cans of food on the shelf and the hot stove made us forget our woes. Chefs Brown and Washburn turned to their task and prepared a good, filling oatmeal-bacon-toast-and-cocoa breakfast. The oatmeal especially was a triumph as it didn't have a single lump in it.

You ought to have seen that food go. A second batch of oatmeal disappeared in no time and then we began to feel full. The dish washers got to work. We all went out and got loads of snow for melting into water and dumped it into the big kettle on the stove.

In a half hour the cabin was as spick and span as ever. All the rubbish was swept out the door into the clouds which rolled by in a warm, never-ending cascade, hiding all views from sight.

At ten o'clock Paul and Dave decided to leave and go down to the Glen. They put on their heavy sheepskin coats and pulled down their woolen caps and set out. We snapped a picture of them through the fog in front of the hut. Then they disappeared around the corner of the Summit House and were swallowed up in the dense mist.

Tappey and Don and I were left with little to do. It was very nasty weather outside and the wind was blowing a real gale (about fifty miles an hour). One minute it would rain, the next minute we would see a spot of blue sky and then it would just settle down and be foggy for an hour. It was the first spring thaw.

We put up a couple of shelves on the wall and then sorted out all our food and figured out that we had plenty to keep us going for a week. Then the blow came. Don's new shoes had given him a frightful blister on his heel. It was two inches long and over an inch wide. His *whole heel* was a blister. We hauled out the first aid kit and fixed it up. It didn't seem to bother him much, because we were going around the hut in bedroom slippers and moccasins so nothing rubbed against it. Just the same, Tappey and I began to worry about it the minute that we saw the thing.

To amuse myself I decided to develop all the pictures that we had taken to date. Tappey and I dug my developing trays, red light, and powders out of my knapsack, and he handed them up to me through a hole in the ceiling as I sat in the low little attic. I arranged everything at the end of the attic where the chimney came up through the floor and gave a little warmth to the frigid room. Two old "two-by-four" boards and a shutter from one of the windows made a wonderful low table. On this I arranged three candle lamps and a red lamp for developing. Then I mixed up the developing and "fixing" fluids and started to work.

It surely was great fun to see our pictures "come out" one by one. There were lots of good ones, too, and all went well until a basin of lukewarm water was passed up to me from below. This peeled the top off a number of pictures and ruined them completely. You see, the water cannot be over sixty-five degrees to develop properly.

About halfway through the morning I got Tappey up to snap a picture of me (with a flashlight) at my developing table. As soon as it was taken I developed it with good water and it was a grand success.

When my work was over upstairs I clambered down by way of

Tappey's shoulders and prepared lunch. We weren't terribly hungry but we ate a good deal just the same. It was just 12:30 when we sat down at the "festal board" to a steaming meal of consommé, peas, and tea. Then, of course, we simply stuffed ourselves with toast and jam which had been the big dish at every meal so far. We had enough bread for a loaf and a half every day for a week.

Developing went on during the afternoon in my workshop in the attic. It is a slow job if you want it done really well. Tappey and Don played cards steadily from the time that Dave and Paul left right through till supper, with short intermissions to get their breath between hands. I have never in my life seen two such card fiends! I finished developing at about five o'clock and came down to see what was going on below.

Don and Tappey were each seated on a hunk of railroad-tie playing solitaire on a bench between them. Their games were upset a bit when I swung down through the hole in the ceiling and landed square on the cards with a crash. Losing my balance I finished my lightning descent by a crash to the floor, carrying with me the whole card game! Tappey told me in plain and simple English what he thought of me for ruining their games which he claimed looked very much as if they were going to "come out." I notice that the games of solitaire that are "going to come out" are usually those which are called off for some reason or other!

Turning a stolid ear to Tappey and his mass of fallen cards I began preparations for supper. I had opened two cans of spaghetti when I decided that the hut was too hot and flinging the door open rushed around the Summit House and back in a mad dash.

When I returned I felt much better for the outing and went on with my supper preparations with much more pep. Besides, this little run had given me the appetite of a hippopotamus. Not satisfied with two cans of food I hauled down some peaches and a "stick" of mushroom soup (at Tappey's suggestion) which looked like a stick of dynamite.

Tappey came over to the table brandishing a big knife and spoon and mashed up the soup, slowly adding water as he proceeded. Don went out for more snow with me and when we returned I cut bread for toast and he stoked the fire and saw to the melting snow.

The peaches were put into a dish, the spaghetti was put on the stove to warm up, the toast was done, and last of all we searched vainly for mushroom in the soup which, to tell the honest truth, might very well have *been* dynamite for all we could taste!

Nevertheless! The supper was a cracker-jack. I have never felt a canned peach slide down my throat with such a cool, filling feeling. It was wonderful. We used up a whole loaf of bread for toast and practically finished one can of jam. It still makes my mouth water to think of that supper.

Dish-washing after a good meal is an anti-climax and it was a terrific one after that meal of ours. The sculch was finally cleared away and the dishes scraped with steel wool, boiled, wiped off, and put away on a shelf.

We spent the whole night up until 9:45 talking over the various merits and demerits of Groton, where Tappey and I go, and St. Mark's, where Don goes. By majority vote Groton was proved the better school. Don and I finally prepared the big camera for some flashlight pictures. I took one of him playing cards and another of Tappey reading *The Canary Murder Case* by the light of one feeble candle, which doesn't show in the picture and hardly showed in the hut. Then by general consent we hit the hay. Tappey and I in hammocks hung right over the stove and Don in the cot in front of it

The temperature was thirty-six degrees outside and we decided to keep really warm all night as we had half frozen the night before. However, we put two extra hooks in the ceiling so that the hammocks could be changed if their place above the stove got too hot. Tappey went out into the dark with a cup of water just before we put out the lantern. Two minutes later he returned with a broad grin. "There has been found in our midst," he said, "an intrepid hero, a dauntless pioneer, a scoffer at restraining precedent! I have brushed my teeth!"

CHAPTER XI

WINTER BREAKS

A yell of disapproval burst from Don and me, the lantern went out, and the hut was plunged into utter darkness. Tappey hauled himself gingerly into his hammock and we went to sleep in a jiffy.

A hammock is a very comfortable thing to sleep in if you get used to it and I got used to mine in about three minutes! The arrangement of the two hammocks was a perfect method (we thought at ten that evening). They were hitched to hooks *directly* over the stove, as I said a little way back, and we had other hooks over the kitchen table and wood-pile to which to transfer ourselves if we got too warm.

When we went to bed it was really rather cold and we thought that the stove position was a splendid one. I slept like a rock till just midnight. A little after midnight I woke up feeling very warm, in fact, very, very hot. I leaned over and looked down at Don in his cot and Tappey in the other hammock. Both of them were tossing back and forth and neither was asleep.

My whole back from the tip of my toes to the end of my hair was roasting! Tappey and I both got down and flung the door open, jamming it with a shovel as we did so. The clouds poured in from outside, bringing with them a refreshing draft of cool air.

What a glorious feeling! I turned my back to the wind and stood outside, with the temperature at about twenty-five degrees, cooling it off in the fog.

Twenty-five degrees may be warm in lots of places but a fifty-mile gale adds to its chill on top of Mount Washington in March at midnight. Two minutes outside sufficed to prepare me for another encounter with the fiendish heat of Camden Cottage.

The open door seemed to have had no effect whatsoever on the temperature inside. It may have cooled it off to about a hundred degrees, but I couldn't tell much difference. I moved my hammock to its emergency wood-pile hook and it felt a lot cooler over there away from the stove, which lit up the whole room with a deep red glow. Besides this, the chimney-pipe had turned a very bright red color and looked as if it might fall at any moment.

We left the door open for about twenty minutes, but the heat in the hut didn't lessen itself a single bit. The only thing that the draft succeeded in doing was adding to Tappey's cold (his hammock's head was right in front of the door) and freezing Don's blistered feet. Accordingly we shut the door and tried to get to sleep, leaving the stove to die out if it ever could.

It was a struggle to get to sleep with all the heat. Nevertheless a half hour or so was enough to do the job, and I didn't wake up again till six o'clock in the morning.

The fire was almost all out and it took us some minutes to get it going again. The hut was icy cold, so we all stayed near the stove till things had warmed up a bit.

At seven o'clock I had gotten my clothes on and we were all hard at work devouring a dandy breakfast of oatmeal, cocoa, toast, and butter. No one will ever be able to imagine how food can disappear until he has seen us three along with a week's supply on top of Mount Washington. Toast disappeared like lightning and oatmeal without cream or milk went down by the ton.

After breakfast was over and the plates and spoons and cups had been cleared away I looked out at the weather. Don in the meanwhile was operating on his blister, while Tappey looked on making wry faces at the awful sight.

The weather looked just as badly as Don's blister did! It wasn't raining. Billows of fog just rolled lazily across the top of the mountains. Now and then the sun glared through for a moment, but all down below it looked black and forbidding. It wasn't going to storm. It was just a plain thaw—heavy low lying clouds full of moisture with a forty-degree temperature in the wind and shade. That is a fairly warm temperature in September on the mountain. In March you feel as though you could go swimming, forty degrees feels so warm.

Nothing but a westerly gale could sweep off those clouds. The wind of the night before had subsided and the air was absolutely still. My five-minute survey done, I strolled in and told Tappey and Don my feelings. An argument lasting some time confirmed my point of view. We decided to "clear out." The frost-feathers were gone and would not return till next February. That meant no more good pictures. The clouds and warmth had melted a really tremendous amount of snow in the last twenty-four hours, and climbing would be treacherous and nasty in the heavy slush that covered the mountain. Get down!

The next question was *when* we should get down. We remembered that a train left from Gorham for Boston at 4:30 in the afternoon. A friend of mine was due on the 10:30 train from Boston that morning. We *must* cut him off and tell him that we were leaving, so that he wouldn't worry if he climbed Washington and didn't find us on top. How would we dry the films? They were still washing in a basin! If I rushed ahead I could make the Glen before the others left for Pinkham and could tell them about our departure. I had just time if I left in a half hour.

Five minutes of that half hour were wasted in sitting on a bench doping out a way for getting down the films safely. Finally an idea hit me and all was well! I cleaned out the raspberry jam jar, filled it with water and carefully poked in our films. Then I screwed on the top and put the jar in my pack to be taken out for drying, when we got to Boston. If it worked it would be the greatest trick imaginable—and it did. Lots of the pictures in this book were taken down the mountain in the jam jar and dried out in Boston.

After the film was safely packed away there followed twenty hectic minutes as we packed up our stuff. The two hammocks were slung up in the attic with all of the cooking utensils in them. Then we closed the hatch in the ceiling and finished packing up below.

My pack was done first and I left Don and Tappey seeing to the finishing touches of cleaning up and stowing away and lashing up pack-boards. It was very warm outside. My heavy boots splashed along through the slush and slid like lightning down the steep snow banks. My shirt collar was the first thing to loosen up. Then I took off my leather jacket and my béret. It was hot work.

Due to our leaving all the food on top, my pack was reduced somewhat, but also greatly added to by Don's incapability to handle a heavy load because of his heel. It amounted to about forty-five pounds.

By running, sliding, and walking I managed to make the four miles to the Halfway House in a little over forty minutes. I stopped there to pick up a load of blankets and other stuff that we had left there two days before. I piled these on top of my pack and changed to my ski boots, lashing my nailed boots to the blankets.

Fifteen minutes was enough. At the beginning of the sixteenth I was starting off down the Carriage Road with my skis on, sliding slowly, scanning the ridge above for signs of Don and Tappey. I caught no sight of them at all and thought that Don might be having trouble with his heel. At any rate I hurried on.

The going was very sticky and I had to use my poles a lot to help me along over the more level of the grades. At the three-mile post I passed a group of people climbing on skis. They wanted to go to the Halfway House. I assured them that there was plenty of room if they wanted it and raced away down their tracks.

The snow in the upward path was so well beaten down that I made fast time from there down and had only one fall. That one was a beauty however! I had to fall carefully in order that the pack wouldn't squash me, and even at that it gave me quite a jerk as I landed.

Even worse than falling was the job of standing up again and hauling on the pack once more. I had slung it on a table to get it onto my back at the Halfway House. Hoisting it from a deep snowdrift to my back was a different matter, and took quite a few minutes to accomplish and I don't yet know quite how I did it.

At 11:45, just ninety minutes after leaving the top and twenty-four minutes from the Halfway House I pulled up panting before the Glen. All my hurry was to no use. My friend had not come on the morning train and Mr. Pike had had no word from him.

Mr. Pike amused himself by pulling my pack apart and weighing it in small chunks on tiny twenty-pound letter scales. I amused myself be devouring all that I could find that was edible. An apple pie, some mutton with gravy and potato, and some tomato soup that Mrs. Pike was getting ready for lunch!—All these fell vanquished before my ravenous mouth.

Mr. Pike told me in an intermission that the load altogether amounted to just sixty-five pounds. It felt like about twice that much and I'll never ski again (I hope) with a pile like that on my back.

Long before Tappey arrived I could hear him yelling and singing at the top of his lungs. He got in forty minutes after me, and Don came up on snowshoes about twenty minutes after Tappey. They had both spent some time at the Halfway House and had been careful of Don's heel above the timber line.

As the car drove us out of the Glen that afternoon and we waved good-bye to Mr. and Mrs. Pike we felt again that a trip does not always have to be a *total* success to have been a success.

———

It was a roasting day in June when our Buick hauled up puffing and steaming before the old Halfway House. Tappey and I and Hal Kellogg, our companion, jumped out. We wanted a short visit to the scene of our winter's night adventure.

We showed a ticket to the man at the door permitting us to use the road. We planned to walk from there to the top and back, as the car might be ruined by the climb and anyway we wanted to get the exercise. The toll-man announced that we had to pay sixteen cents each for walking up the last four miles of the road. I paid the forty-eight cents and not till now did I realize that he really only ought to have charged us twenty-four cents, as we only walked up half the road and had paid for the car for the first half. I'll collect that twenty-four cents on my next trip!

During our conversation as we looked over the "dear old house" the toll-man happened to catch the words that we had spent a night there last winter. At this he exploded into a long bawling-out of us and all our kind for leaving the hut in such an awful mess.

We protested that it had been left spic and span from attic to foundation, but he refused to believe us. In fact he said everything that he could about us, except for saying that we had stolen something.

After a few minutes of this clash I retired to the front porch to look up the mountain. It was hard to realize that only three months before that ridge had been such a scene of roaring rushing snow. It was *just* three months before that we had climbed the peak, and I could still see the snow lashed furiously across that treeless, bare ridge where now only a couple of small patches of ice remained, melting fast in the eighty-five-degree temperature.

As I was still looking at the height above us Tappey came out and we started up around the Horn. He was bubbling over with laughter and when we had turned the corner a little above the house, he burst into a roar of mirth. The man had asked him why we had taken his "TOLL COLLECTED HERE" sign (forty pounds) and left it hidden in the woods, ten feet up a tree.

Tappey's reply had been short, clean cut, and to the point. "Why should we have taken your blasted sign out of the house at midnight in the middle of a blizzard with well over ten feet of snow covering that tree? I can tell you what, if we had found that sign, we could have split it up and used it for firewood."

Roars of laughter echoed form the cliffs above us. Tappey had certainly baffled the toll-collector and we climbed gaily onward up the road under the roasting sun, all the time recognizing spots at which we had nearly frozen to death three months before! There is nothing like looking at a spot where once you have been in misery.

Our trip was crowned with a sun-bath, stripped to the waist, lying on the rocks of the road (just below the summit) where our packs had fallen off. On that June day Tappey and I encountered in the heat and breathlessness of the air the very equal of last winter's combat with the snow and wind. The summer is beautiful in the mountains. Winter is to be dreaded, fought, and feared, never to be trifled with. But the winter every time for me!

The Fairweather Crew. Left to Right, Hodges, Olson, Kraetzer,
Washburn, Batchelder, and Emmons.

BRADFORD ON MOUNT FAIRWEATHER

BY

BRADFORD WASHBURN

ILLUSTRATED WITH PHOTOGRAPHS AND
SKETCH MAPS BY THE AUTHOR

*To Bob Morgan, a fellow mountaineer
whose constant and unselfish work on our plans
is deeply appreciated by the author.*

CONTENTS

PHOTOGRAPHS

CHAPTER I

OFF FOR THE NORTH

laska! The word alone thrills us with the glamour of exploration and adventure. Thousands of miles of unexplored
rivers, vast expanses of virgin forest, glaciers, gold mines, pack
trains—all these flash through our minds at the very mention of
that magic country.

Many of us have read the famous epic of Alaskan mountaineering: *The Ascent of Denali* (the Indian name for Mt.
McKinley), *The Ascent of Mt. St. Elias*. The Himalayas of India
alone come near even equaling the snowy grandeur of the
Alaskan ranges. Nowhere else in the world, with the exception of
the Polar Ice Caps, do we know of such expanses of snow and ice.

Mount St. Elias (18,002 feet), at first believed to be the highest peak in North America, fell to a party of Italian mountaineers
in 1897. In 1913 Denali or Mount McKinley (20,300 feet), the
true monarch of North America, was conquered by Hudson
Stuck, Archdeacon of the Yukon, after any number of other expeditions had struggled unsuccessfully to climb that tremendous
peak. Mount Logan (19,539 feet), the second highest mountain in
North America, held out until 1925, when an intrepid party of
Americans fought their way to its top through hardships such as
no climbing expedition has ever known.

With these giants all climbed, one might think that it would be hard to find another big mountain in Alaska. Quite to the contrary. With the exception of these three ascents, the three great ranges of Alaska have scarcely been touched. Of the McKinley Range, Denali alone has been climbed. The interior range has yet seen but little exploration and Logan and St. Elias are the only peaks of the Coast Range to have fallen prey to mountaineers.

Out of the hundreds of beautiful peaks that still remain untouched by man, probably the most beautiful is Mount Fairweather. Although by no means the highest of the unexplored horde (15,330 feet), Fairweather is marvelously protected on every side by barriers of rock and ice such as few mountains in the world possess.

Situated in the center of a chain of peaks called the Fairweather Range, fourteen of them higher than ten thousand feet, Mount Fairweather lies on a narrow peninsula jutting southward from the coast into the gulf of Alaska. It is less than twenty miles from ocean tidewater to the west and about twenty-three miles from Glacier Bay on the east.

Fairweather was first known to have been seen by Captain Cook on one of his world voyages towards the end of the 18th century. From that time on it is an uncommon occurrence for a ship passing Cape Fairweather on a clear day to neglect making some remark on the beauty of this range that rises nearly as high as Mont Blanc and much higher than the Matterhorn right out of the ocean.

Until 1926 the ascent of the mountain as far as I know was never attempted by anyone. In May and June of that year the first bona fide trip on the mountain was made by Dr. Ladd and Allen Carpé of New York, accompanied by Andy Taylor, a guide from McCarthy, Alaska. Although two of these climbers were veterans of the Logan Expedition of only the preceding year and the third is well known for his mountaineering ability, the party was forced back at slightly above 9000 feet and admitted when they returned that Fairweather is no ordinary 15,000-foot mountain.

Bob Morgan, a member of the Mount Logan Expedition, and one of my closest friends, happens to live in Cambridge. One evening last January, while at his house, I chanced to run across an account of the 1926 attempt. We skimmed through the short article and glanced at the four small pictures, merely remarking that there was a big chance for exploration still open in the Fairweather range.

Several weeks later we happened to be together again and somehow or other the subject of Fairweather came up. We talked it over all one evening and decided that some day we should try to climb the mountain—some day in the far future. But, having nothing better to do and knowing the value of plans made a long time in advance, we spent many enjoyable February evenings counting up probable costs of a trip to Alaska and listing up food and equipment.

Finally, after nearly a month's planning and deliberation, the inevitable question came. Why not this summer? Nobody else was going out this summer. We should have the whole field clear for climbing and exploring. I knew a man interested in our enterprise and especially in the pictures that we might get.

Long letters and talks and trips to New York followed and by the end of February I was surely going north to attempt Fairweather, to get movies and still pictures, and map this unexplored wilderness of snow and ice.

Many more days were spent choosing the "Fairweather Crew," as we called them. Bob could not make it. Business kept him back in Boston, but he kept on working with me. One by one we got the men. They were chosen not for their ability as mountaineers but for their power of mixing well together and for their knowledge of back packing, cooking, and camping. Art Foote, a classmate at Harvard, was my first man. Then we got Gene Kraetzer and Dick Hodges, both of them with several years' experience as packers for the Appalachian Mountain Club Huts. Art Emmons, another Harvard classmate, followed and by the middle of March the whole crew was completed with Ken Olson from the Harvard Medical School, a fellow with five years' experience guiding on Mount Rainier.

Even while the crew was being chosen, Bob and I kept on with the planning. Equipment was being ordered steadily all through

March and at the same time we struggled with the greatest bug-bear of all expeditions—the food.

Every expedition about which we read seemed to have had some trouble or other with the kitchen. Usually there was too little food—in one case there was far too much and at the end of that trip the climbers found that they had packed over a thousand pounds more than necessary.

Something must be done so that we should not need even to think about the food; so that every day our only care should be the load that we must carry to the next camp; so that if we were beaten it would be by the mountain and not by our own unpreparedness.

The method that we struck upon was the "food bag" system. It took days and days of minute figuring. Bob and I spent long evenings in actually eating and comparing several different brands of foods in order to have the best possible and the brand from which we could get the most food with the least weight. We would sit down at a table in Bob's little kitchen with pen and paper and cook the food to be tested. Then we would multiply by three the weight of the kind that we chose and finally add a little, because a man packing ten miles or so out in the open each day needs much more food than a housed-up city man.

We began with lists of all the food that we liked while camping. We divided these into breakfast, lunch, and supper lists and then sub-divided those into different menus so that we should not have to eat the same kind of food each day. Then we weighed out the food by days and, figuring that we should be able to stay on the mountain for only fifty days, we multiplied by fifty and got the total amount of each thing we had to order. If you get mixed up while reading this, read it over once again and realize that Bob and I had to read the lists over till we nearly went mad before we could get them ready for ordering.

But finally the great day came and ordering lists went out to grocers all over Boston and Massachusetts. Dick Hodges and I carried home more than 700 pounds of food in one load in the rumble seat of my little Ford roadster. Then when the food was all under our roof and the bags had been labeled, we set to work packing them. One pound of sugar went in a little parafined bag in each big daily bag, 12 bags of tea, and so on until they were all packed. The only things that we carried in bulk were salt and pepper. They always went along with the cooking utensils and gasoline stoves. Each bag was complete from A to Z. We never could "run out" of anything because the same amount was waiting untouched in tomorrow's bag. Even the butter was canned and put in, and each bag had a can opener, a dish towel and a box of steel wool.

The daily bags were numbered from one to fifty and put in pairs in twenty-five heavy canvas container bags, so that they would not get badly mutilated or leak with rough handling.

This solved the food problem for good. We allowed sixteen days' food (eight coming and eight going) for the base camp at the sea and bought a pile of miscellaneous food for those days, since we did not need to back-pack it and weight could be disregarded.

It takes just a few moments to tell about this work and just a few pages (see page 227) to show all of the lists, but it was the 2nd of May before the last bag had been boxed up and was off for the North.

We did not plan to start till June 13th and a whole month loomed up ahead in which we could rest and exercise and prepare for the great trip. On the 25th of May the personnel received its first and only shock. Art Foote, my first man and right-hand partner in the Expedition, got appendicitis and could not go. Scarcely two weeks and we were to leave!

A wild week-end followed in which Dick and I drove all over Vermont, Massachusetts, and New Hampshire and finally nailed the man that we wanted to fill Art's place: Ralph Batchelder, or Batch, as we all called him, a veteran hut-man and packer for the Appalachian Mountain Club.

Examinations were the next hurdle to be leaped. In all my life I cannot recollect such a terrible pair of weeks as those first two in June. Amid frantic efforts to study, the telephone was constantly ringing, telegrams were being exchanged at frightful cost in attempts to find whether the baggage had arrived at Juneau, the capital of Alaska, and I was making almost daily trips to Bob's home clearing up our last lists and plans.

On the morning of Friday the Thirteenth of June—a fatal day for a superstitious person—a group of five excited fellows were gathered at the North Station ready to leave for Alaska. Ken Olson had gone home to Seattle and was to meet us on the boat which we took from Prince Rupert, B.C., to Alaska.

Tickets, checks, porters, baggage-mixups, good-byes and a million little last minute errands were finally completed and, sitting on the observation car, we saw Boston fade into the distance.

One roasting day followed another as we crossed the plains of Canada and then the Rockies and the Coast Range. Ken was waiting for us at Prince Rupert on the *S.S. Prince Rupert*. The crew was all together again and we had a grand handshake all around. Ken had not even heard about Art Foote and so Batch and he met for the first time on the dock at Prince Rupert.

That afternoon and all the next day we spent in the most delightful cruise on which I have ever been. The boat follows a passage northward between the mainland and the long, thick chain of off-shore islands that extend from Seattle all the way to Cape Spencer, fifty miles south of Mount Fairweather. We wound in and out between the islands now close to their wooded slopes, now below the snowclad peaks of the Coast Range, rising five and six thousand feet out of the sea. Some of the islands seemed so near that we could almost touch them.

In the mid-afteroon of the second day (June 19th) we steamed up to the head of Taku inlet, where the great icewall of the Taku glacier drops 300 perpendicular feet into the sea. The whistle of the boat made several wild toots to try to loosen some of the fine pinnacles of snow-sculptured ice by the vibrations of the air. Nothing fell till about ten minutes after the whistling had stopped and then several great chunks boomed off into the water with a tremendous splash and floated away as icebergs.

Two hours later the *Prince Rupert* was on Gastineau Channel. The little town of Juneau, nestled close under the steep walls of Juneau Mountain, lay just to our right. A dark cloud hung low over the houses, the smoke and dust from the Alaska-Juneau

Mine perched high on the hill behind the houses; the gold mine with the largest daily output of any in the world. The mountains drop so steeply into the water that most of the town is either built on a forty-degree slope on the side of the hill itself or on piles out over the water.

After a hasty supper aboard the boat, we landed our equipment and loaded it aboard the 34-foot gasoline power-boat that we had hired to take us to Cape Fairweather. And then at nine o'clock in the evening, in that beautiful northern twilight glow that lingers so long into the night, we cut loose and started for Cape Spencer and the Gulf of Alaska.

Dick and I sat on the bow alone and speechless as we glided over the mirror-like waters of the channel, past the rotting remains of the old Treadwell mine—one of those Alaskan ghost towns—once the richest gold mine in the world, now deserted, the bay caved in on the shaft and the buildings falling to pieces.

As we gradually got further and further from Juneau and the roar and clatter of the mines died out and the twinkling lights began to fade away in the mist and smoke, I turned over in my mind all that had happened in the last few months. How the whole thing did seem like a dream—those long plannings with Bob, those terrible days packing food, and the weeks of waiting to go. And now here we were in Alaska at last and only a day and a half more from the mountain.

CHAPTER II

A BIT OF BAD LUCK

At crack of dawn Dick and I took the helm and Ken, Gene, and Bill (the boatman) went below to sleep. When we came on duty the boat was chugging along at its slow but sure six miles an hour, headed for the entrance of Icy Strait—a stretch of water, entirely interlocked by islands, leading to Cross Sound and finally Cape Spencer and the Pacific, now only eight hours distant.

I've never seen the sea so calm. With the exception of occasional tide rips, its surface was as smooth as glass. We took turns steering and cooking ourselves breakfast and by six o'clock we were well out into Icy Strait. It was there that we got our first view of Fairweather, still over fifty miles away, but looming up huge and white and pointed, mirrored on the surface of the water. La Perouse, Crillon, and Lituya, the three smaller peaks south of Fairweather, seemed even larger and more beautiful, they were so much nearer, their snowy slopes almost meeting the water directly ahead of us.

All morning we crossed the Strait over water without a single ripple disturbing its surface. Early in the afternoon we put in at the big salmon cannery at Port Althorp to get reloaded with gasoline for the 75-mile run up the Gulf of Alaska to Cape Fairweather. Then we put to sea again at about three o'clock and headed out into Cross Sound towards the Ocean.

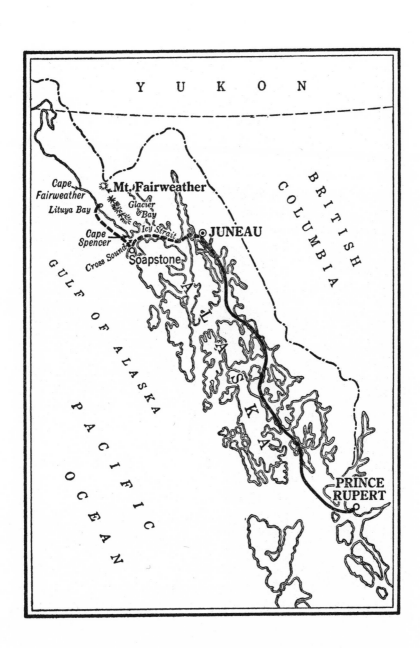

Y U K O N

BRITISH
COLUMBIA

Cape
Fairweather
Lituya Bay

Mt. Fairweather

Glacier
Bay
Icy Strait

JUNEAU

Cape
Spencer

Cross Sounds

Soapstone

GULF OF ALASKA

A
L
A
S
K
A

PACIFIC

OCEAN

PRINCE
RUPERT

Good luck seemed to have followed us so far every step from Boston. Now the tables turned a bit. As we entered the sound a long ground swell from the southwest began to toss our little peanut shell of a boat to and fro. A gentle breeze from the same direction was stirring up tiny whitecaps atop each wave and after a half hour of rolling and pitching about we saw a light fog streamer coming in toward us from the sea.

There are only two harbors between Cape Spencer and Cape Fairweather—Dixon Harbor and Lituya Bay. The first would be nearly impossible to find in a heavy fog and the second, if it were found, has a navigable entrance only two hundred yards wide that you can only enter at slack tides (either at full high water or at complete low water), because of the terrific speed at which the tides flow in and out of the narrow channel at its mouth.

It would be jumping right into the lion's mouth to start out up the Gulf of Alaska with such definite signs of a southwester in the making. So we swung our bow around a little more to the south and put in at a Soapstone inlet, a sheltered cove right at the mouth of Cross Sound. We planned to wait there till the weather looked more promising.

The U.S. Government maintains a radio compass station at Soapstone for helping ships to locate themselves and, after we were safely anchored and had had supper, we put the dinghy overboard and rowed ashore to pay the operators a visit. There were three of them. They lived in a comfortable white frame house on the shore of the inlet and every day each spent an eight-hour shift at the instruments in the lookout tower, several hundred feet up a hill behind the house.

We all climbed the hill and the men showed us their instruments. Later on we clambered up the tower. From it there is a stunning view of all Cross Sound and the coast to the north as far as the spits at the mouth of Lituya Bay. On the other side of Cross Sound and directly opposite us rose the massive ramparts of Mt. La Perouse, the southernmost peak on the Fairweather peninsula.

The weather was still unsettled, even though the sky behind the mountains was a gorgeous sunset pink. Streamer of fog still persisted in floating in over Cross Sound and a bank of leaden clouds hung low to the southwest.

A wait that we first expected to be overnight drew out to one day and then two and on the morning of the third the weather still looked very lowry. Every hour or so we'd have a little squall of wind and rain and then some more fog would blow in from the sea. We spent most of our time ashore. Dick and I studied the geology of the cliffs at the Point for the report that we were to make to Harvard in the fall. Art and Batch hunted and Ken and Gene fished.

The game seemed to play in droves just ahead of us, but nobody ever got anything. On the second day the fishermen gave up after trolling for a couple of hours and joined forces with the geologists and hunters in an eagle hunt of great magnitude. Leaving the boat and fishing line and geologic axes and notebooks at the beach, we scrambled up a gully in the cliffs all full of thorns and brambles. A long search finally revealed an eagle's nest at the top of a large, very prickly pine tree. Ken volunteered to climb it and after a terrible tussle he emerged victorious at the nest, torn and scratched from head to foot. It was absolutely empty.

When he got back to earth again, thoroughly disgusted, we all went out to the crest of the cliff and there, right below us was a school of fish so thick that they were jumping out of the water. It was exactly where the fishermen had been only an hour before.

A half hour later, when we got back to the boat, an eagle with at least a six-foot wing-spread sailed right into Ken's nest!

A duckling, all feathers and too small to eat, hit by a stray shell from Batch's gun, was the only game that the three days at Soapstone netted!

On the morning of the 24th of June we got up at four o'clock and started on a fourth try to get to Lituya Bay. Once there we could be in calm water and beautiful scenery. At a moment's notice we could put to sea from there at be a Cape Fairweather in two hours and a half. With a murky sky overhead and a greasy southwest swell we crossed to Cape Spencer and passed the Spencer lighthouse at nine o'clock after a two-hour run against the tide.

Once beyond the cape the weather seemed to clear a bit where we were and to get blacker and more ominous everywhere else. We sailed past Icy Point at exactly noon under a perfectly blue sky with black clouds about us in every direction. The mountains were buried deep in fog.

About an hour after passing Icy Point a fresh northwest wind began to pick up. The La Perouse Glacier comes right down to the sea at this spot and breaks off into the ocean with an ice-front a good 200 feet high. The wind added to the southwest swell and the backwash from the ocean splashing against the cliff of ice set up a bad chop.

Bill, who is a decidedly nervous skipper and a terrible pessimist, was almost on the point of turning back and laying over another day in Dixon Harbor, that we had just passed, right near Icy Point. But by urging him on to tell us his life history (which was very long and varied), we managed to get the boat through the chop and nearer Lituya Bay than Dixon.

That, we considered a great achievement. The swell let up and the chop stopped as soon as we passed the glacier, but the breeze kept getting fresher all the time.

We continued to keep the seas off our port bow till we were opposite the narrow spit that lies across the mouth of Lituya Bay. Bill, we discovered at this spot, had never been through the channel except once thirty-five years before. We had several minutes yet before slack tide, so we got out a book and read up the way to get into the bay.

Nine men, we discovered, were drowned when the first attempt to enter the bay was made one hundred and fifty years ago. Any number of mortal accidents have occurred since then. It seemed that the place that looks most obviously safe in the gap through the natural breakwater is really the most dangerous. You must "stick within seventy-five yards of the Cormoran Rock," the book said, "and then, following the current, you can't help getting in— never try to get in on an ebbing tide, as it may prove too much for you and carry you into the breakers off the rocks."

That all sounded fine enough, but the tide was already beginning to flow in at the entrance and where was Cormorant Rock?

The whole mouth of the bay was lined with gigantic boulders. We chose the biggest rock in sight and headed seventy yards west of it.

The current was flowing even faster that we had expected and before we could realize it we were whisked through the narrow entrance by the rocks and into the beautiful calm lagoon beyond. I heaved a sigh of relief that seven more men weren't yet added to the Lituya Bay death list.

CHAPTER III

THE PLANS ARE CHANGED

L ituya Bay is a deep trench extending six miles from the sea to its head, far back in the mountains. It was formed by a huge glacier, now long since melted away, which gouged its way through the soft rock where the bay now is and piled up rock debris at the end of the ice where it dropped off into the sea.

Gradually this piling up of rock made the natural breakwater around the mouth of the bay, and, as the glacier melted away, a portion of rock not quite all worn off was uncovered. This is now called Cenotaph Island. At the very head of the bay are the two stumps of the old glacier. They have both stopped receding and, if anything, are advancing a little again.

The tides in the bay are very queer and hard to plan on unless you know that they are *two hours later* than the tides outside. The entrance is so narrow and shallow that, although the water races in like a roaring torrent with the tide, it is unable to fill the bay even with the sea till the tide outside has reached its height and has actually ebbed for nearly two hours.

Going out of the bay it is always safest to wait till the tide is coming gently in and buck it out. The worst that the current can do in that case is to carry you back into the calm bay. If you try to get *in or out* with the tide ebbing, once in the entrance you are at the mercy of the outgoing current that makes a tremendous chop where it meets the incoming ocean swells.

In short: the Lituya Bay entrance is a very delicate spot to negotiate, and if you miss your chance to get in you will have to fight the sea outside the entrance till the tide changes, with no refuge nearer than Dixon Harbor, thirty miles to the south.

So it was with a load off our minds that we glided up the bay to Cenotaph Island and dropped anchor late that June afternoon. The trip from Soapstone had taken exactly ten hours and forty-five minutes.

The chop had been so nasty off Icy Point that we had had very little lunch and we ate a whale of a supper, all seven of us huddled around the tiny table in the cabin.

Jim Huscroft, an American prospector, who came North some years ago, lives on Cenotaph Island, where he raises blue foxes for the fur market. He and his partner, Ernie Rognan, who is out on the gulf fishing most of the year, have built a couple of log cabins at the west end of the island right near where we anchored. We went ashore after supper and met Jim, who happened to be entirely alone at the time.

He expressed his grave doubts about anyone's being able to land at all anywhere near Cape Fairweather because of the heavy breakers along the beach. He also voiced his opinion that the best way to start was up the glacier at the head of the bay and to follow it northward twenty miles behind the coastal hills till we reached the base of the mountain. This would be at least six or seven miles longer than the way straight to the mountain up the Great Plateau Glacier that ends only one-quarter of a mile from the ocean at Cape Fairweather.

The 1926 party had landed at Sea Otter Creek, six miles north of the Cape, but we had started too late for that route, since it followed a glacier said to be badly crevassed after the middle of June, when the winter snow had melted away from its surface.

Despite Jim's warning, however, we decided to go on and at least get a look at the Cape before making such a big change in

The *Typhoon* Anchored at the Head of Lituya Bay.

the plans. If we *did* have to go in at the head of the bay it would mean probably the better part of two weeks or ten days time lost, according to our original schedule.

As far as getting to the *top* of the mountain was concerned, the situation was decidedly dubious. Our old plans left a margin of plenty of extra food—the new one would mean virtually no time to spare. The last boat south left Juneau on August 30th—that would mean being back at Lituya Bay on our boat by the 23rd or 24th at the latest to give the weather a safe allowance for getting back on time. Besides, when we sat down to figure it out, we found that our fifty days food would only last us till the 22nd of August anyway.

Fairweather was playing a tricky game. She had us with our backs to the wall almost before the start. It was not only the mountain that we had to climb, but we had to fight the ocean as well.

The next morning we left the bay on the eight o'clock tide and started toward the cape. The weather was as clear as crystal. Only the slightest breeze rippled the surface of the heavy swells and Fairweather, majestic and white and glittering, towered high

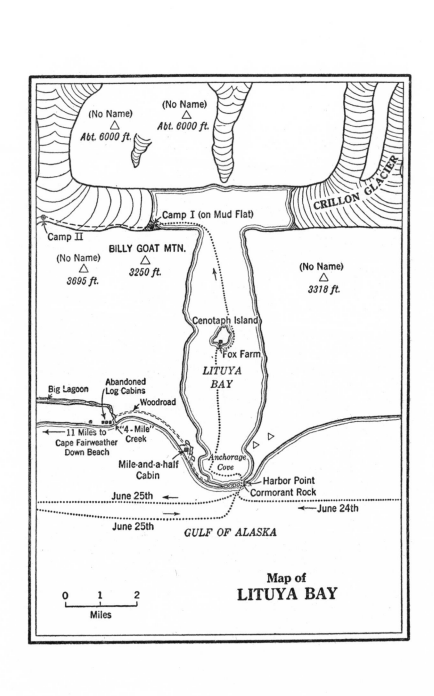

(No Name)
△
Abt. 6000 ft.

(No Name)
△
Abt. 6000 ft.

CRILLON GLACIER

Camp I (on Mud Flat)

Camp II

BILLY GOAT MTN.
△
3250 ft.

(No Name)
△
3695 ft.

(No Name)
△
3318 ft.

Cenotaph Island

Fox Farm

LITUYA
BAY

Abandoned
Log Cabins

Big Lagoon

Woodroad

←11 Miles to
Cape Fairweather
Down Beach

"4 - Mile"
Creek

Mile-and-a-half
Cabin

Anchorage
Cove

Harbor Point
Cormorant Rock

June 25th ←

←June 24th

June 25th →

GULF OF ALASKA

Map of
LITUYA BAY

0   1   2
Miles

above the blue of the ocean and the green of the range of low coastal hills.

The breeze got heavier and heavier till it really would have been called a wind and by ten o'clock whitecaps began to appear. When we got opposite the end of "Fourteen Mile Creek," where the Great Plateau Glacier empties into the sea, it was clear that no boat could land there unless under exceptionally calm conditions, and even then it would probably be a very risky job. Where the creek flowed into the sea there were terrible waves and tide rips and to both sides of the creek there were four distinct separate lines of breakers combing in on the beach. Then and there we changed the plans.

Turning sharply about, we sailed along in the trough of the waves, occasionally taking a small sea aboard. Although a good long way off, Lituya Bay got near very quickly on the way back as the seas boosted us onward. When we got opposite the entrance, the tide that we had left low in the morning was still pouring like a whirlwind through the narrow crack in the reefs, great sheets of spray dashing far up onto the rocky shore.

In the meanwhile the waves outside the bay were beginning to get a bit nastier and, as we ran back and forth waiting for the tide to slack up, the old boat took some pretty fine seas over her bows. At noon we decided it much safer to ride the current in than wait outside another hour, so the skipper, Gene, and I stayed in the cockpit and the hatch door was closed fast.

We spun the boat around once more and headed her for the harbor mouth. According to the book we were absolutely safe, but in for a rather rough ride. The nearer we got the worse things looked! The current was just roaring through that entrance as the ocean struggled to get in and fill up the bay.

Three cormorants sat on our big rock sunning themselves as the water lashed all about them, and I wished for once that I was a cormorant or a rock or *anything* out of that boat! As we approached the tide rip, a low roar of water could be heard. The flowing water was several feet higher than the rest of the waves about it and we aimed right for this rushing mill race.

At last we were in the current—a million times worse than it had appeared from a mile offshore. Swept along with eddying waves and whirlpools flecked with foam, we were carried toward the bay mouth. In a second the boat was in the apex of the rapids. Several seals flashed by, fighting the current and catching fish in the swirling water. They, too, looked happy and calm.

It was all over in a second, just as the book had said, and before we realized it we were inside the lagoon, wiping the perspiration from our brows and opening the deckhouse door.

What a ride. You can be sure that we'll never go within a mile of that gap again at anything but slack water, no matter whether the ocean outside is in a hurricane or not!

The boat anchored in the lagoon and after lunch we walked four miles up the coast and back in one last attempt to see whether it would be feasible to land or even to pack our stuff along the beach. From the good level sand the ocean looked calm offshore, but the breakers still rolled in. It was hopeless—hopeless either to land or to pack along the beach. The waves were too much of a risk—the sand was too soft. It would prove much easier to go Jim's way—a way that Bob and I had always had in mind as an alternative if the first way for some unknown reason should fail. Now the reasons were staring us in the face.

Late in the afternoon we turned the boat toward the head of the bay. After supper we put on our climbing boots and walked a mile or so up the glacier to choose a route for our first pack. At first the going was very rough, but after about three-quarters of a mile the trench along the west edge broadened out and was filled every now and then by big hard-packed drifts of winter snow. The going there was good and it looked as if it would continue for some time, so we called it a day—it certainly had been a terror—and hurried back to the boat and bed.

We'd reached the start of the long climb. From now on we must fight every minute to get our supplies through to the mountain, in one big effort to get there soon enough to make it.

CHAPTER IV

DESOLATION VALLEY

O n the morning of the 26th of June we put up the big nine-by-twelve tent on a gravel flat at the end of the glacier and spent the morning filling it with supplies and arranging them in piles. We ate aboard the boat and went back to the tent after lunch. There we loaded up our first packs to average between forty-five and fifty-five pounds. Our plan was to start light and then gradually work into heavier loads getting into condition as we worked, rather than trying to start off with very heavy loads and burn ourselves out before we had got any reserve force built up.

We used several different types of frames or pack-boards on to which to lash the packs. Ken and Gene had "Trapper Nelson" boards, I had a Yukon board and the other three used Nash pack carriers. The latter were decidedly the lightest (four pounds), but did not fit one's back nearly so well as the other two. The Yukon is the heaviest (six pounds), but had the advantage over the others of being able to pack a load so high that the point of balance is at your shoulder and not in the small of your back. The Nelson boards had a bad way of falling to pieces and always in a difficult place—there was some little thing wrong with each kind, but each man swore that his board was the best.

It was about two o'clock that we left Camp I and started the grind up towards the second camp. The route up to Camp II was one of the meanest packs on the trip. It was necessary to follow the very edge of the glacier all the way. For the first few hundred yards one's life was really in peril from rocks that slipped off the crest of the glacier and slid into the trough up which we were packing. We usually stationed a scout who watched for rocks and the rest hurried up by the danger spot. Then they watched while he rushed along.

After this death trap in which nobody ever got even a scratch there followed a half mile of terrible bush-whacking among alders through which it took some time to wear a trail. Then came piles of moraine—the rock loosened up by a glacier at its edges as it moves along like a great plow share. The first few trips over this, too, were very tiring until a trail had been worn. Wading ankle deep in loose rock that turns under one's foot at each step is far and away the most fatiguing part of the trials of a packer.

After the first hour was over and the trough filled with hard snow reached all went well. We plodded slowly on till we saw ahead what appeared to be a height of land or col, as it is called in mountaineering language. A glacier poured in from our right and flowed both towards us and away from us, parting at this height of land.

That was the obvious place for the second camp. Another hour's work and we came puffing and blowing up over the last snowfield onto the col. It had taken over three hours from the bay up and we were glad to throw down our loads and cool off.

At what we estimated to be five or six miles further to the northwest another glacier flowed out from the east side of the valley, precisely as did the one opposite our present position. It seemed to do just what ours was doing—to pour out across the valley till it hit the other side and then split and flow both toward and away from us. Between us and this far glacier there was a depression several hundred feet deep into which these two halves flowed. They seemed to meet there and the ice not to flow either way in the deepest part of the hollow.

We had carried up two small seven-by-seven tents and enough food and gasoline for stoves for three of us for four days. Dick,

Batch, and I stayed at Camp II that night, since the weather looked as if it would hold good for one day more at least. We'd get away early the next day and go all the way into the hollow, over the glacier in the distance, and on as far toward the mountain as we could. If possible we'd try to find places for the next two camps and mark the route ahead. Then, when we arrived at Camp II with our last load, there would be no delay in starting work on to Camp III even in case of fog or rain. This was the famous Polar Camp System; always pack up from the camp at which you are sleeping—never go down for your loads, for in that way you are packing the food that you are eating.

My remembrance of the first two nights spent at Camp II, pitched right on a snowfield, are none of the best. Once we got into the swing of the game all went well, but at the start it was pretty rough.

We started at four o'clock the next morning. The fog had settled down over the ice in a thick blanket. We were forced to walk for four hours on the compass bearings that we had luckily taken at sunset the evening before. The first hour and a half was downhill over heaps of gigantic boulders strewn over the surface of the ice, then the grade lessened and, before long, we began to climb up again slowly but surely.

We were beyond the hollow and going up the other side of it. Now the ice was almost smooth with only a rock or two on its surface here and there. At eight o'clock we reached what seemed to be the place where the second glacier poured in from the right. The ice ahead of us dropped slowly away and was lost in the fog.

Coming to a little pile of rocks we sat down and decided to wait till the mist should rise. All beyond us was new country that we had been unable to see from Camp II. Absolute silence reigned about us. Fog and snow were all that we could see and the fog was so thick that we could scarcely make out rocks fifty feet away through it.

I stretched out on a big boulder and closed my eyes. The next thing I knew it was nine o'clock and I heard Dick calling faintly, "Look!" We had slept nearly half an hour and the fog had entirely melted away. A beautiful, smooth snow-covered glacier lay for miles down the valley and, to the right, just ahead it seemed, Fairweather's great snow dome peeked out from behind a wisp of morning mist.

Three more hours of fast walking down the snow and then along the level and we were at the Plateau Glacier, up which our old route from Cape Fairweather would have come. That was surely the place for the fourth camp. Now we must find a good place for the third. We were about eleven miles from Camp II. The ridge where we had had our nap appeared to be about halfway, so we turned and started back, this time following the west edge of the glacier in an attempt to find the very best route on which to pack.

Here and there we built cairns or piles of stones a couple of feet high to use as landmarks on future trips. We located a fine camp site on some rock-strewn ice right at the height of land and built a big cairn at it. Then, speeding off towards Camp II, now visible in the distance, we covered the five miles in two and a half hours.

Ken and the others had just arrived with a load from Camp I and we told them the lay of the land. It was clearly such a long way to the bottom of the mountain that we must cut down on all supplies and take only bare necessities outside of food.

We all returned to Camp I and the next morning sorted out the equipment once more. In the afternoon we packed another load through to Camp II.

The nine days of packing out of Camp I and then the five more from Camp II to III are a nightmare as I look back at them. It seemed as if we'd never get through those terrible moraines above the bay. And finally when we did get everything to Camp II it rained every single day that we worked from there to Camp III. Every night we'd peel off a layer of dripping clothes and hang them on the line outside. It was raining hard when we did it, but the things couldn't get any wetter and there was a chance that it might clear up. Every morning we'd wring the water from our socks, squeeze into soaking boots, and start off again.

It was no use to put on dry clothing. It would be wet in ten minutes. In five minutes the torture of putting on wet socks was all over and our feet warm again. My boots, that weighed three and

The Geologists at Work on the Cliff Behind Camp II.

a half pounds before getting wet, weighed nine and a half pounds together with two pairs of wet socks after a day's run to Camp III.

We called it Desolation Valley. Both sides of it were bare walls of rock with scrubby alders alone hardy enough to stick to the crevices. The floor of the valley was ice covered with rocks. Pack, eat, and sleep was all that we did. Occasionally we'd get back to camp early on an exceptionally cold day when we could not rest much as we packed. Then we would play cards or sally forth onto the slopes of the west side of the valley in a lull in the rain to get some alders for firewood. It was never very cold in Desolation Valley, but it wasn't ever very hot either. The coldest reading we ever had was 44 degrees, but the warmest day or night was 52 degrees!

Even the smoky blaze of green alders lent a cheery atmosphere to the camp and we used to sit before the fire and sing and talk about home, dry clothes, and baths and fresh food till the wood ran out and we had to crawl into our sleeping bags for the night.

CHAPTER V

STARVATION CAMP

W hat a relief it was when we shouldered our last load out of
Camp II and, leaving a bag with two days' food for the
return journey, started toward Camp III for the last time. Dick,
Batch, and I had had a day off after our twenty-two mile recon-
noitering trip. The others had packed steadily without a break for
fourteen days with the average load now creeping nearer sixty
than forty pounds.

The sun came out as we left Camp II and, slipping back and
forth between the clouds, it stayed with us till noon. Then the
good old mist came in and the clouds settled down once more.
Dick and I crossed the eastern edge of the glacier and went up that
side of the valley till the hollow, then crossing back to Camp III.
This side trip, that proved to be terribly tedious wading through
moraines and along loose rock slopes, was made so as to have a
better chance to study the rock formations and ice on that side of
the valley for our geology report.

Geologizing six miles with a sixty-eight-pound pack on your
back and pockets bulging with rocks is no tea party, I can assure
you! After we had picked up the old pack route in the hollow and
followed it to Camp III, we were thoroughly winded. The others
had gone by the regular route. They had already got the big tent

The Route Below Camp III Still Covered by Winter Snow.

up and were rigging the nine-by-twelve tarp up in front of it as a sort of awning. Dick and I sat and watched them, leaning against our packs, eating lunch. We cleaned up half a package of Vegetized Wafers, a whole box of nearly fifty sardines, and a dozen dried apricots each in about ten minutes. After that we felt like new men.

A little tent was set up beside the big one to use as a protection for general supplies. Along one side of the awning we heaped up all of the food bags and then piled the air mattresses up against this wall. That made a grand sofa. Three big rocks, tilted one against the other, made a fireplace in front of the sofa, the only trouble with it being that as the rocks got heated they gradually sank down into the ice!

Camp III certainly was a de luxe layout when we went to bed that night. But one thing was missing. If you have read the food lists in the back of the book you will remember that Klim (powdered milk) is to be found in *every other odd bag.* We had left bag No. 5 at Camp II to use on the way back. That meant no Klim for four days. We had found that the canned butter was all rancid at Camp II and that had been somewhat of a blow. We had three two-pound cans of butter to last six men for six weeks! No butter and no milk—that was too much. Nevertheless, we would a million times rather die of hunger than go back to Camp II after the milk! So then and there we named Camp III, "Starvation Camp."

A fire there was a luxury, for to get wood it was necessary to climb down a steep, rocky slope, cross a gully, and climb up a hundred or more feet on the other side to reach the willow thickets. Once cut, the wood had to be dragged back roped in bundles. An ice chest for our precious butter (only one tin remained now, one having been lost and the other eaten at Camp II) was the least of our domestic problems, a small hole chopped in the ice floor of the tent serving the purpose perfectly.

But the packing situation here was a much tougher one than we had just been through. The going was only fair at first over moraine scattered on the ice and then along more snow patches at the edge of the glacier. It was a very long grind—a good six miles—and the slushy snow at the end never failed to soak our

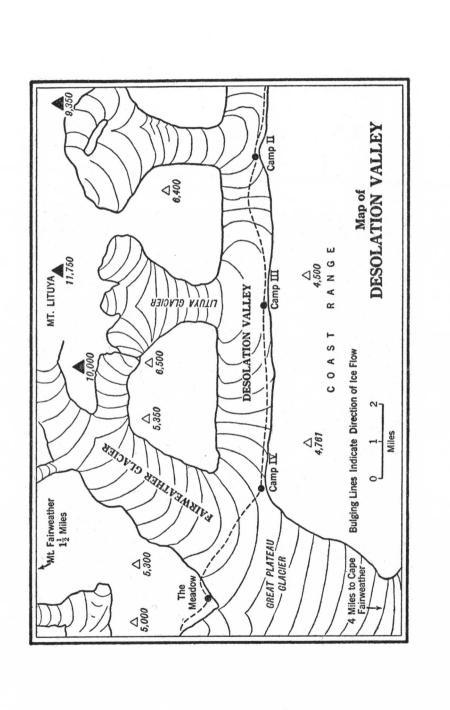

Map of

DESOLATION VALLEY

Bulging Lines Indicate Direction of Ice Flow

0   1   2
Miles

feet just as badly as had the rain. No boot grease could keep you dry. Once the top of your socks were wet it seeped down irre-sistibly through them into your shoes—your feet had a daily bath at any rate.

On the ninth of July, the day after we got to Starvation Camp, a day-off was proclaimed for all but Ken and myself. We got an eight forty-five start and reconnoitred the pack route to Camp IV. It had changed quite a good deal since Dick, Batch, and I had been over it. A lot of the winter snow had melted off and bare ice was left for nearly a mile in one spot.

We had lunch at noon at the end of Desolation Valley seated on a steep moraine overlooking the Plateau Glacier. It certainly was a great expanse of ice and, from where we were, appeared absolutely flat and uncracked. We saw Fairweather for a moment through a gap in the mists above us. It had not actually rained yet, but the clouds hung low, within a few hundred feet of the surface of the ice.

Ken left the tent where we had lunch and we set out across the Plateau Glacier towards the base of the mountain at exactly twelve twenty. Usually a glacier when seen from a distance looks much smoother than it actually is, but the Plateau Glacier is a glaring exception to the rule.

At the edge of the ice we took a compass bearing on the other side of the glacier. The ice was as flat and smooth as a pancake and in fifty-five minutes we had gone the whole three miles across it and were nibbling a bit of chocolate on the opposite moraine.

After a few moment's rest we climbed the steep bank of rock and peered over the other side. I have never in all my life been so surprised as I was just then. Instead of the barren heap of rocks that one finds on the other side of most moraines there was a beautiful meadow. Its surface was a good thirty feet below the crest of the moraine on which we stood and was triangular in shape, each side being at least a mile long. The glacier outside was so low and the moraine so high that it had been quite hidden to us until we nearly stumbled on it.

The meadow was fringed with evergreen trees that grew on the steep inside slope of the moraine which bordered it, and the ground was deeply blanketed with blue lupine over two feet high and heather and cyclamen and any number of other kinds of flowers.

We scrambled down the slope to the level grass and almost at once struck a well-beaten bear trail. It led us around the lower end of the meadow that sloped gently towards the corner furthest from the mountain. At the point of the corner a wonderful brook of clear, fresh water came down the fields from our right. It roared through a narrow canyon it had gouged out of the meadow's moraine barrier, and rushing over a falls, disappeared under the glacier outside.

It was such a queer contrast—this terrible all-powerful ocean of ice flowing by outside—the peaceful, quiet meadow with its flowers and thrushes and only separated from each other by a thirty-foot pile of dirt and trees.

The bear trail was so well worn and led so exactly in the direction in which we wanted to go that we kept following it, singing loudly now and then and yelling at every blind corner to keep any of its rightful owners well ahead of us. About one and a half miles along this trail led us all the way around to the far northern end of the meadow. There we climbed the moraine again and looked around.

A glacier a mile or so in width lay ahead of us, flowing toward the Plateau Glacier, which it met at the falls at the end of the meadow. It was so covered with rocks and dirt that the ice itself was nearly hidden—a sign that there were very bad rock avalanches up near its source on the great mountain.

The other side of that rock-covered glacier was the very base of Fairweather. We slid down a good sixty feet of loose rock and gravel inclined at a very steep angle and got onto the ice then, wending our way back and forth between boulders we crossed to the opposite shore.

So many wonderful things had happened that I could scarcely imagine what we were in for when Ken reached the top of the opposite moraine and sat down with a loud exclamation.

If you have ever tried to climb up a heap of loose gravel or sand you have a fair idea of what a struggle it is to get up a sixty foot moraine. Wading and slipping and showered by pebbles and rocks from above I finally struggled out onto the top and stared.

Behind this moraine was a narrow, V-shaped valley. The inner slope of the moraine was overgrown with grass and alders and a black, mysterious virgin forest, fading away into the clouds, rose steeply on the other side from a dry brook-bed in the bottom of the V.

It was raining and a cold, wet breeze was coming down the little valley toward us. Continuing along the crest of the moraine we climbed to the lower edge of the clouds at a height of about 2000 feet. There the moraine ended abruptly. The glacier had gotten so steep that it had turned into a veritable cascade of ice. It now flattened out again and a broad plateau of snow-covered ice extended as far back as we could see below the clouds towards Fairweather.

The summit was now straight ahead of us, but we must gain the top of the ridge to our left before the upper reaches of the mountain could be explored. We had gone our limit, however. Several gullies disappeared into the clouds toward the ridge, but there was no use going further. We had already come nearly fourteen miles and would have to go all the way back to Camp III. Besides the clouds were so thick and the rain so cold and nasty that it was scarcely possible to see a thing.

It was a long, long way home; five hours steady walking with only one short rest at the meadow and another at the site for Camp IV. When we got into camp at eight forty-five that evening, just twelve hours after our start, we were mighty glad to get a good hot supper and roll into our bags for the night.

Ken and I had a day off the next day. Gene, Dick, Batch, and Art took a load ahead to Camp IV, piling it at a place where we had made a high cairn the day before.

There were only two striking occurrences at Camp III besides the milk shortage which forced us to eat our Bran Flakes with sugar and water.

Our route to Camp IV passes beside a huge pond about a mile long and several hundred yards wide, made of melting water gathered in a hollow on the ice. On the third day of packing we had got some very beautiful moving pictures of packing along the edge of the water. On the return trip the same afternoon I noticed that a ridge had appeared in the middle of it and that it was now a pair of smaller lakes.

Art and I had stayed late at the Camp IV supply heap or "dump," as the pile of equipment gradually accumulated at the end of a pack is called. It had been especially clear weather, in fact the first clear day since the 24th of June, and we had gone out onto the Plateau Glacier to get some pictures. Returning to camp late in the afternoon we saw a large block of snow under the awning. On it was the fresh imprint of a bear's foot—not a very big bear, but then it was a good ten inches from tip to tip.

Batch had found it 300 yards from camp. A tremendous brown bear had also been sighted across the gully near the alders where we got wood.

We decided that there must be bears from all over the mountain rallying for an attack on our camp. If we had been hunters we should have welcomed the intrusion, but all of the artillery had been packed through to Camp IV that morning, so we were plenty glad that Camp III was to be broken the next day.

On the following morning as we packed down the ice towards Camp IV we discovered that the lake had *entirely vanished*. Nothing but a deep trough with a big crevasse in its bottom showed where the great pond had been.

CHAPTER VI

THE ICEFALL

S tarvation Camp disappeared behind us—the further the better. It had been a damp, chilly spot at best and not a speck better than Camp II, with the one fact excepted that it was nearer the mountain.

Camp IV was scarcely a camp at all. After a hasty lunch at the dump we lashed on new loads, all over sixty and three of them heavier than eighty pounds. These we carried the three miles across to the meadow. Art and I, determined to have less work on the following day, carried two sixty-pound loads on a second trip the same afternoon and left them two-thirds of the way across the ice, planning to pick them up the next morning.

Camp IV was a makeshift camp pitched on the ice at the end of Desolation Valley. Fog rolled in up the Plateau Glacier from the sea. The rain came down in torrents all night. Our socks were soaked, our boots were filled with water. The dufflebags were drenched—*everything* was dripping when we got up the next morning.

After breakfast the fog lifted a mite. We cleared up everything and scrapped camp. We left six days' food here for the return trip, but even at that, the loads were very heavy. Batch, Ken, Art, and I each carried over a hundred pounds. But it was all over in an hour and a half. A good rest on the other shore and Art and I came back to get our loads left part way the day before. The rest went back to Camp IV for another load. Dick and Gene had to make three round trips.

By supper time the tent was up, a roaring fire was going and the mattress sofa had been rebuilt. Camp V, or the Meadow Camp, as we called it, was in the most beautiful location of any camp on the trip. Nestled in a little hollow in a corner of the meadow, it was pitched on a carpet of deep moss and surrounded by perfect oceans of blue lupine.

Fresh brook water was the joy and blessing of the meadow. At all the previous camps we had struggled to find little glacier ponds or to melt snow. At Camp III we had chopped a deep hole in the ice beside the tent and the melting ice always kept the hole full of water. At the meadow the brook flowed right by the tent. We could have the privilege of a real bath if we wanted it.

I awoke early the next morning before anybody else was up. The weather had cleared off. Above us, to the east, rose a peak we called Mt. Holmes after Burton Holmes, a backer of the expedition. A lovely pennant of wind-driven cloud was flung out to the north of its snow-capped summit, framed by the evergreens of the meadow. Dew sparkled with the sun on every tiny leaf of moss and lupine. It was like fairyland come true.

Three days that we spent packing from the meadow over to the final base camp in the gully on the other side of the rock-covered glacier have for me the most beautiful remembrances of the whole summer. Then we moved on to the base camp.

The hollow that had once appeared cheery to Ken and me proved to be a veritable den of mosquitoes. An Alaskan mosquito put beside our eastern domesticated insect is about like an eagle beside a sparrow. The Alaskan species know all of the ins and outs of biting and they usually travel in droves (at least so it seemed) with the black flies. The mosquitoes reigned supreme at night, the flies by day.

Mosquitoes were the subject of discussion most of the night. One of the longest drawn-out arguments on the trip—and a trip of this sort has many long arguments—was among Gene, Ken, and Dick as to whether or not a mosquito can navigate in the rain. Gene claimed that they could navigate between the drops in a light shower, but none were ever seen abroad after the first few drops.

After bedtime we swore all night in no lenient manner at the little beasts that used to swarm around our netting and whirr till they nearly drove us crazy. I think that the reason why Alaskan prospectors swear so vehemently is because of their constant training with the mosquitoes for years on end.

Despite the mosquito menace we made the base camp a comfortable place in which to live. We built a log framework eighteen inches high on which to set the tent, thus making the three-foot wall four feet six inches in height and just doubling the standing room inside. Then we built a huge fireplace and stretched the tarp out in front of the tent as we had done at Starvation Camp and the Meadow.

On a day off the hunters began to show a little enterprise, too. A grouse fell after Dick had peppered four shots all around it in the undergrowth. A young mountain goat weighing thirty-five pounds came home on Art's shoulder. The food for the next two days was above all our highest hopes. The grouse turned out to be larger than a big chicken and fed us all for one meal, besides making marvelous soup for the next day. The kid first gave us chops and then, later, liver and kidneys. Starvation Camp was forgotten in our exultation.

Trouble was ahead, however. Gene, Dick, and I climbed from camp to the ridge twice in one day in an attempt to find the best gully for packing purposes. They were all frightfully steep, the most gradual slope of any being nearly forty degrees. Only one was at all feasible for packing and only light loads could be carried up that. It led straight from the smooth upper Plateau of Nichols Glacier (the rock-covered glacier, named after Dr. Harry P. Nichols, a great lover of the mountains and a friend of all of us), straight to the crest of the northwest ridge of Fairweather, reaching the ridge in a very jagged notch at 4950 feet.

The site for Camp VII was chosen on a snowfield just on the other side of the crest of the ridge in a wonderfully sheltered spot.

Owing to the very long summer days and the hot sun the north side of all of these mountains is very much more snowy than the southerly one which gets the sun nearly all day long.

The beginning of the gully was a good two-hour pack from the base camp. So to lessen the difficulty, we packed all of the equipment necessary higher up to a dump about halfway to it. Even at that the climb was 2000 vertical feet with a steepness varying from forty degrees to spots that were quite vertical.

On the 20th of July I chose Dick and Art to go ahead to the next camp with me for the night and make a thorough reconnaissance up above on the following day. We figured that after all necessary equipment was packed to Camp VII there would be food accumulated there for fourteen days further work. If the route that we had chosen in Cambridge should offer any great setbacks there would not be sufficient time left to make the top.

Accordingly we all set out with packs averaging some thirty-two or thirty-three pounds each. The first half of the gully was snow and we made good time up it despite its steepness. But the second half was exceedingly steep and all full of loose rocks. The last man up kicked loose as many as possible so as to safen future trips. The first five climbers had to take care not to brain each other. So the going was snail-like and it was not till later in the day that we made the ridge and pitched the seventh camp. Enough clothes, food, and gasoline had been taken for four days and one small tent was put up.

The clouds were down tight all about us. We might just as well be camped on an icepan in New York Harbor in midwinter for all that we could see of the mountain. After supper a light rain set in. There was nothing to do but go to bed, so to bed we went. The alarm clock was set at 2 A.M., but when I poked my head out at that ungodly hour, all was still fog and rain.

At eight o'clock, however, it cleared and we rushed through a short breakfast. A silvery-topped sea of clouds tossed below us out over the ocean. We roped up and started off at nine thirty after a careful examination of the steep, crevassed snow slopes that mounted above the camp. I led, Dick was second, Art third.

We had picked the route out so carefully before leaving camp

Putting Up the Base Camp.

that we had scarcely had a single setback all the way up the big slope. At eleven o'clock we reached a rock islet at the top of it. There we had lunch. The sea of clouds, now far below us, was gorgeous beyond words. Ever rising and falling, twisting and shining, its beautiful surface slipped quietly along toward the south. It was just like a brook, eddying around the mountains and, when it came to a low, dome-shaped hill it would roll right on over it, burying its crest in glittering mist.

Lunch finished, we climbed a short, gently rising snow-slope that had hidden the upper part of the mountain from our view all day.

I was the first to reach its top. I stopped short as if stunned. The other two came up beside me. We looked for several moments, only the dull roar of ice tumbling somewhere in the far distance breaking the silence.

A tremendous ice cliff four hundred feet high and absolutely vertical rose but a few hundred yards ahead of us beyond a level snow field. To the right were rock cliffs rising nearly vertically for a good 2000 feet. To the left of the ice crag a glacier a half-mile wide flowed out of a valley of smooth snow a thousand feet above. At the end of the valley, most of which was hidden from our view, the glacier swept past us, seething in one of the grandest icefalls that I have ever seen.

The way was blocked.

CHAPTER VII

BACK TO THE BASE CAMP

What an icefall! Pinnacles of blue and green ice capped with white snow, great walls and blocks of ice, towers of ice; all came tumbling out of that valley in one endless cascade that flowed past us and out of sight beyond a nearby shoulder of snow.

We crossed the flat snow between us and the cascade. Even this was cut up by tremendous crevasses. I'll never forget one of those holes. Seeing it quite a distance ahead, I told Dick to keep close track of my rope. A snow bridge about eight inches wide and twelve feet long was the only means of getting across.

As Dick watched my rope, letting it out bit by bit, I slowly ventured out on the narrow crossing. The snow was so soft that I sunk in nearly to my knees at the first step, a great chunk of the bridge tumbling away into the darkness below. Each step from then on I carefully packed with my foot before moving ahead. The seven or eight steps to the other side seemed to take a year. Once I glanced down to my right. The beautifully colored walls of ice went straight down on each side, turning gradually from light to dark green, deep blue and then inky darkness. Of all the crevasses that I have ever seen, that was the most terrible.

As we neared the icefall the crevasses became more and more frequent and finally we were in the cascade itself. Only three hundred yards of work showed that the task was colossal. It would take several hours of continuous labor to hack a way across to the other side through this sea of broken, piled-up ice. And then, for what use? It would be impossible to pack loads to higher camps through such a mêlée.

The only remaining possibility was the ridge on the other side of the icefall. It was steep, but smooth right from the bottom to within a short distance of the snow valley above the cascade. But to get to it the cascade *would have to be crossed*.

At two in the afternoon we had another lunch and on our descent toward Camp VII we carefully scanned the cascade to see if there was such a thing as a way across it anywhere. A really thorough search showed us that the only possible crossing was at a point 4000 feet high (900 feet *below* our camp).

The afternoon mists were rolling in as we returned to camp. Ken, Gene, and Batch had brought up another load from below. After a few words with them they plunged into the fog that still lay below us and started down the gully toward the base camp.

That night late we discussed the situation. Our route was blocked. A descent of 800 feet would be necessary to strike a route that would lead us a least to 9000 feet. Above 9000 feet a big notch existed in the ridge and from there to the summit appeared to be distinctly tough going—a sharp, steep snow ridge. When the equipment had been packed through from the base camp only fourteen days of food would remain. That would have to take us not only to the top but all the way back again to the base.

These were the facts and we talked them over and looked at them from every possible angle. The top could be reached in fourteen days from where we were, but that would only be possible if we had continual good weather. Besides it would be impossible to work steadily up such steep slopes without at least two days off in fourteen. And then, last but not least, a nine hundred foot descent in the middle of our line of camps would be a very dangerous handicap if somebody got hurt high up on the mountain.

At 2:30 A.M. on the 23rd of July we cooked breakfast and started for the base camp. It was gloriously clear outside. Not a cloud was in sight anywhere and the stars were already beginning to disappear at the end of the short Alaskan night. Tiny banks of morning fog scurried to and fro, here and there across the dark face of the Pacific Ocean that stretched out like a great plain 5000 feet below us.

Roping up we started down the gully and in two hours were at the base camp. The fellows there were just getting ready for an early day's work. And, sitting down with them to a steaming pail of corn meal mush, we talked the future over together.

It was finally agreed that the time had come for us to turn back. It was a great disappointment, but the chance for the top was really awfully slim. The risks of so hurried a campaign would be great. All weights would have to be cut to a minimum and we couldn't possibly take along any moving picture apparatus.

From every point of view our trip would be more of a success if we returned to the lower camp and continued our exploration of the base of the mountain for the next ten days or two weeks. It would be a lot better to go home loaded with knowledge and pictures of the region and in grand health than to stake everything in a risky struggle for the top and return worn out, with nothing to show for our work.

A load off our minds, we climbed back to the ridge and spent the rest of the day taking movies and still pictures of the camp and icefall. Then, late in the afternoon, we gathered everything together and packed it up. And, saying farewell to the icefall, we started down our gully for the last time.

Packing loads *down* a gully we found to be quite a different proposition from going up, especially since we had two loads each to take down all at once. Only three men could work at a time because of the great danger of falling rocks. So Art, Batch, and I took light loads and went ahead and the three others stayed to let the stuff down with rope to the glacier below.

At ten o'clock at night, Ken, Dick, and Gene tumbled hot and exhausted into camp. What a tale they had to tell about getting down that gully. Dufflebags had broken loose and gone bounding down for hundreds of feet, lodging at last on narrow ledges. The ropes had gotten tangled in the rocks. The tent poles were lost. They had three heavy loads with them. The rest of the stuff they had left halfway down the gully when darkness fell and they couldn't see to gather up our unfortunate equipment that was strewn from one end of the gully to the other!

A red hot supper put new life into them and in an hour we were all sound asleep back at the base camp again.

CHAPTER VIII

PARADISE VALLEY

The next morning I was awakened by the whirr of black flies. I twisted and writhed to try to get my mosquito netting fixed right. I'd rolled out from under it during the night. After a hopeless struggle with the tangled netting I gave up and wriggled out of my sleeping bag.

The sun was shining brightly. What a chance! I dug out the little parafined bag that contained my toilet articles and had a general washup, followed by a shave and a good rub with talcum powder and cold cream. Then I set to work to cook breakfast.

We ate at nine thirty and spent a quiet day around camp, practically all that we accomplished being a re-rigging of the tarp that served as a roof for our front porch. By using one of the little tents for a wall and spreading the tarp more tightly we almost doubled the size of the porch. After supper we spent a good long time in preparing our headnets and fixing them securely on for the night.

The next day we went up to the gully and while Dick, Gene, and Ken got the loads that they had left halfway up it we took movies of them from the upper plateau of the Nichols Glacier.

On the afternoon of the following day Batch and Art went up to one of the ridges above camp and Ken and Gene went after a last load to take down from the cache halfway to the base of the

gully. Dick and I set out down the edge of the Nichols Glacier on
a trip for geology and mapping.

We followed the moraine for some distance and then when we
got opposite the end of the Meadow, instead of turning left we
swung sharp to the right and turned into a glacier valley, really a
continuation of the one that we had packed along from Camp I
to Camp IV. After climbing up and down for some time over the
rolling surface of the rock-covered ice we came to a mound a little larger than the rest.

It seemed as if we'd never stop having surprises. The
Government map that we had been using showed the place where
we were as a wide ice-filled valley. Before us lay over a mile of dirty
ice. In the distance we could see the tongue of the Carpé Glacier
as it crossed the valley that we were in and flowed on toward the
sea. But between the two glaciers was a beautiful lake, stretching
the whole width of the valley and nearly two miles long.

Following the glacier we hurried down the slope toward the
lake. Although it had looked almost at our feet when we first saw
it, it was a good half hour before we reached the end of the ice and
looked out over the lake.

Its waters were that lovely shade of greenish blue so typical of
ponds filled by glaciers, but Paradise Lake as we called it was more
beautiful than any lake I have ever seen before. On the two sides
of the valley the steep wooded slopes dropped into the water with
scarcely any suggestion of a beach and, at the further end, the
edge of the Carpé Glacier rose in a sheer hundred-foot cliff right
from the surface of the lake.

But it was getting late and we must hurry to get back to camp
by supper time. We crossed to the west side of the glacier and on
the further slope of the moraine found another tiny wooded valley just like the one at the base camp. On the way up this we
found several places where gold might easily be panned from the
brook-bed gravels. We took some samples of the gravel and then
continued up the brook-bed.

An hour of climbing up this gully led us back to the Nichols
Glacier again, so we climbed up to the top of the moraine. In the
little valley below us, and slightly ahead of where we had just

The Lower Part of the Gully. Three Figures Are Visible Halfway Up.

been, were three more ponds, all very small, still they were beautiful and must certainly go on the map.

Sitting atop the moraine with a small instrument I sighted the angle of all the main points up and down the valley. Dick copied them down in his notebook and then we took a series of pictures of the lakes and the glaciers to help in drawing up the map when we got back to Cambridge.

It took just over an hour for us to cross the glacier and get back to camp and there we spent the evening telling the crew of what we had discovered. The hunters had forgotten all about their job and had spent the whole afternoon lying on some rocks far up the hill behind camp above a sea of clouds trying to get a good sunburn.

We had quite a lengthy council of war before we went to bed and decided that we'd spend one more day at the base camp and then move on towards Lituya Bay. We also discussed the best route back and finally chose the way by the Plateau Glacier to the sea and then to the bay along the beach. That was to have been our old route in and we were all eager to get a chance to see new country on the way back.

Early on the morning of July 27th the party again set out on voyages of discovery. Ken and Gene, quite overcome by our stories of gold sand, were eager to get a chance at panning in the creek that Dick and I had found the day before. Art and Batch paired up to go across the meadow to do some exploring on the Fairweather Glacier. Dick and I were both for going to Paradise Lake again and seeing the country to the west of it.

We all set out at 8:30, Art and Batch to the east, the rest of us toward the west. It only took us about an hour to get far enough to show Gene and Ken where the gold was to be had. Then we split up again, Dick and I aiming down the valley toward the lake, and the others with a packful of frying pans and a pick, going to the gold fields.

We followed the edge of the Glacier about as far as Paradise Lake. Just before we reached the water we struck off to the right over the moraine and tried to get to the north bank of the pond. The alder bushes gradually got thicker and thicker and the ground became muddier till in about ten minutes we were picking our way through a swamp that would make the Great Dismal Swamp look like a four-ply concrete highway.

Literally swimming through alders, mosquitoes, and oozy moss we at last forded a rushing stream and reached the side of the valley. A ten-minute scramble through the virgin forest on the steep slopes of the valley wall and we began to strike fresh sign of bear. We had no gun and the undergrowth was so thick that a bear would have had no trouble at all in getting a mighty fine dinner of us, so we plunged through another field of alders and came out on the lake shore. There, if worst came to worst, we could at least give the bear a good swimming race before his dinner.

After looking up the lake it seemed as if we were in for a swim, bears or no bears! The bushes came down so near to the water that there was no possible way of following the shore. It was a question of get wet or go home. We chose to get wet.

A good gravel beach ran out from the shore for about ten feet. It was all about two feet under water. That served as our roadway for the next half mile, and it wasn't till then that we realized how really wet our feet had been back in Desolation Valley! Even a half-mile walk in water ranging in depth from our knees to our hips didn't seem to make them feel a bit wetter than they had been in those moraines three weeks before.

At last we struck dry land again and a good rock beach led us a mile or more to the end of the lake. There we followed a sandy flat to the edge of the Carpé Glacier, climbed to the ice, and crossed it till we struck a good place for lunch.

Perched on a huge cone of rocks in the very center of the glacier we ate a grand meal of cheese, apricots, crackers, and chocolate. I made a complete panorama with the still camera from the peak rock of the cone and we got another set of angles for our notebooks. Then we set out westward once more.

We were now crossing the glacier that the 1926 expedition had climbed from the sea in their ascent of the great icefall. The clouds hung low over the mountains, but we got occasional glimpses of the icefall as we continued along the valley.

Yesterday having found a lake not on the map, our purpose today was to find that one shown on the map didn't exist. Only

Taking Motion Pictures of the Icefall.

two miles after our lunching place we reached a fine hill of ice from which we could see the valley for a good ten miles ahead. There wasn't a single speck of a lake in sight and, what was even more, a wide strip of woods crossed the valley a mile or more below us. On the map the whole valley had been shown as continuous ice. We'd found not only a lake crossing it in one place but a whole forest a little further on.

That was all that we could do. From where we were we could see as far up the valley as we could walk in five hours, so we turned and started back, the way that we had the day before, on the west side of the glacier.

There was one question about the way back and that was whether or not we'd find it possible to pass the lake on the southwest side. That remained to be seen, but we were willing to do nearly anything before we went through the wading ordeal again.

The going wasn't nearly so bad as it had looked from across the lake. A fine gravel beach led all the way to the far end. At two places where little cliffs came down to the water we had to climb the slope to get around them. The lake must have been terribly deep because the bottom was invisible from the top of those cliffs and the beach on which we were walking shelved off steeply only a few feet from shore. I noticed several little fish in the shallow water near the shore. How on earth they even got there is a mystery to me. The only outlet of the lake that we could find was at the western end and entirely underground! The water was as cold as ice and little bergs from the Carpé Glacier floated about at the west end of it. That half-mile wade will stick in my mind a long time as one of the coldest dips I have ever had.

Back on the good old Nichols Glacier again we made fine speed and were at camp in time for a big supper at six in the evening. Paradise Valley was at last thoroughly explored and photographed.

CHAPTER IX

THE MARCH TO THE SEA

Tough as may have been the work of packing in along Desolation Valley, the march to the sea across the Plateau Glacier was tougher. Our loads were infinitely heavier and we traveled daily routes a third again as long.

The day after our trip up Paradise Valley we shouldered fifty-five-pound loads and walked more than halfway from the Base Camp to the sea, a distance of about eight miles as closely as we could figure it from walking time. A big forested point of land juts far out into the ice at the spot where we left our loads. The glacier, as it flows around this corner, plunges over a ninety-foot cliff of rock, then flowing in a gradual slope to its end only a quarter-mile from the sea at Cape Fairweather.

It would clearly be necessary to rope our gear down over the cliff when we got it all together at the top. It would be far too much of a job to attempt starting that job after an eight-mile pack and with eight miles still to return before bed.

Accordingly we made the best time that we could back over the fairly smooth surface of the Plateau and the wild chaos of moraines at the end of Nichols Glacier.

The Base Camp was broken the next morning amid the frenzied buzzing of a billion black flies and mosquitoes evidently delegated to give us a send-off such as no Alaskan campers had ever seen before. In Alaksa the one way to get camp broken in a hurry is first to pull down the tents and roll them up. That's all that is necessary. The black flies do the rest. A man just can't stop working and moving amid the swarms of flies—he just simply *has* to hurry.

We planned to move everything over to the Meadow in two loads and then to pack it through from there to the Point in two more. All of us agreed that an eight-mile pack and an eight-mile return were far too much of a workout to repeat three days in a row!

Each man was allotted a pile of equipment to take to the Meadow and each took it in his own way. Ken, Batch, and Dick took two complete round trips; Art and Gene first took a load each over the Nichols Glacier to the corner of the Meadow. Then they took a load all the way through to old Camp V and finally came back for their load left halfway. I went with Gene and Art on their first trip, but halfway back on the second lap I lashed my first load on top of my second and took the whole pile into camp at once— a rather gruelling, but much the shortest method of procedure.

What a relief to be back in the peace and charm of the Meadow once more! The lupine still bloomed on as blue and lovely as ever. The thrushes sang and the clear, cold brook roared out through its gateway to the glacier. This time camp was pitched at this gateway and a good two hundred yards from the old Meadow Camp. The new site was much nearer the brook and we all got a grand washup, Dick and Ken even taking a dip in a deep pool. But they yelled so loudly when they ran out of the water and their teeth chattered so long that the rest of us chose the time-honored and much more soothing sponge-bath system.

A load went to the Point early the next morning in about half the time it had taken us to put it through from the Base Camp because from the Meadow we got right out onto the Plateau Glacier and avoided all of the Nichols Glacier moraines.

In order to speed up operation for the next day we had an early lunch and roped all the supplies down over the cliff to the level glacier below. It had been wonderfully clear all day, the Pacific standing out a brilliant blue in splendid contrast to the white glacier and the fringe of evergreens along the shore at its tip.

The last night at the Meadow passed like a flash and we were off for the sea at last. Ken and Gene had a big job ahead of them. They were to start before us and take two light loads to the Point and then return four miles to Camp IV and take the three food bags that we'd left there all the way through to the sea. We were to take one heavy load (seventy pounds) to the sea, stopping on the way to rope Ken and Gene's first packs down the cliff to the dump at the bottom.

The clouds hung low over the ranges all day and a still lower level of mist blew up the Plateau Glacier from the sea, so that we were forced to travel the last two miles above the point entirely by instinct—that is to say by noticing the curves of the crevasses and the moraines till it seemed the right time to turn left to the edge of the ice and reach the cliff.

Our "instinct" on this particular day happened to be excellent. We reached the cliff in just three hours from the Meadow. Lowering the loads over, we ate lunch at the bottom and then started for the sea—still a good four miles distant.

But the ice of the lower glacier was even smoother than that above the cliff. It was all strewn with bits of slate that lay with their flat side up. Two hours of almost steady walking brought us to the tongue of the Plateau Glacier. It was there that the good going ended.

A perfect sea of alder bushes grew in a layer of dirt and moss actually on the surface of the ice and completely covered the last mile of the glacier tongue. Our route wound back and forth through these alder forests and between mud flats and pools of stagnant water.

The twelfth mile of a pack with a seventy-pound load is none too pleasant on flat land, but tossing back and forth amongst this shrubbery was a rough finish. I can remember falling at least twice and having to wait until Dick could come up and pull my load out of the bushes before I could stand up. He, too, took some nasty falls.

Finally we burst through a dense thicket of alders and came out on a wide sand flat at the end of the glacier. Ahead of us ran a torrent that was quite impassable. We set down our loads and walked down the bank a short distance. Our campground lay on the

Fairweather from the Sea Camp.

beach only a quarter mile away beyond the stream. But there was the stream, surging, roaring up from under the ice—made of every drop of melted ice water from the whole valley that we'd just come down.

It was a good hundred yards across and in an attempt to ford it we were nearly whisked from our feet by the sweeping force of the muddy torrent. The quicksands around the end of the ice were frightfully treacherous. We both fell in at least once, well up over our boots.

As we were discussing the lay of the land, Art and Batch, who had been a little behind us all they way down, came out onto the sand flat. We told them that we were going to try to find a way over the river by crossing the tongue of the glacier and then coming down on the other side of it.

So we left them resting on the sand bank and, without packs, began to bush-whack our way across the tree-covered ice without packs. Right up on the center of the glacier the going was just beyond words. The alders were inter-grown with prickly dwarf spruce trees and devils club—a terrible western plant with a stem about as big as a sunflower's and pithy branches all covered with large prickly balls.

The fight across that narrow tip of ice was the most terrific that we had all summer. Just halfway across I stepped into a hornet's nest. Dick screeched "hornets" at the top of his lungs and we both began to run as hard as we possibly could. I don't know how we moved at all. The brush was just as thick as anywhere else, but we ran as if the devil were at our heels and covered as much ground in thirty seconds as we had in the twenty preceding minutes.

But that dash lost us our direction and in a few moments we were only a few hundred yards from where we had started. Having made a perfect circle, we were now looking right down on the sand flat again!

There was nothing at all to do but turn right around and start back again. Our thirteenth mile is a nightmare to me still. We kicked and pulled at bushes and scrambled over piles of loose rocks, and at four in the afternoon we reached the south edge of the Plateau Glacier. Such a scene of desolation I've never before seen in all my life. Huge fir trees uprooted by the moving ice lay spattered with mud along the piles of granite blocks and loose dirt that bordered the edge of the ice. Pools of muddy water surrounded by twisted, dead alder bushes lined the trench between the moraines and the glaciers.

By following this confusion for ten minutes or so we came to the creek. This time, however, we were on the right side of it. When we reached the narrowest spot we found that Art had discovered a way across where the current wasn't bad at all.

With three fellows on each side we had very little trouble in throwing a line across the stream. We'd brought no rope at all down from the cliff, so we had to use one of the pack-board cords. It was exactly long enough and two fellows held the ends tightly while the others took the loads across, wading waist deep in the icy waters.

A quarter of a mile down the rock bank of the torrent led us to the beach where great combing waves were rolling in from the Pacific. The march to the sea was over!

CHAPTER X

THREE LITTLE HILLS

The Sea Camp was pitched a hundred feet from high tide level, right on the beach, and roped to several old driftwood logs. A big log in front of the tent that faced the sea served as a back to our fireplace, a rousing blaze of wonderful dry wood blazing in it most of the night to keep bears away.

We might almost have called this "Bear Camp." It was located at a sort of Times Square of bearland. The only fresh water for miles up and down the coast was the creek that came from the bottom of our glacier and the bears literally came down in herds to drink there every night.

Although we were nearer the animals than we had been at any time before on the trip, we never saw a single one at the beach camp. They always came down to drink at night, leaving a trail in the sand scarcely fifty feet from the tent. They were the Alaskan Brown Bear, we were sure, because they are a common animal along the coast. You can tell their size very accurately by the size of the footprint. They are as long in feet from tip to tip as their footprints are long in inches. The footprints behind the camp ranged anywhere from eight to fifteen inches in length and parallel to the big, deep trail was a smaller trail made by the little cubs as they capered around on the sand following the mothers.

The Sea Camp had all the advantages of a boat without any of the failings. I loved to lie on the couch of mattresses, far back in the interior of the tent, and watch the ocean rolling in only few feet from the door. The sensation of being on the deck of a boat was quite perfect, but the horizon was so nicely fixed in one place that we never had a qualm of seasickness.

We spent a day of complete rest on the beach the day after our twelve-mile hike down from the Meadow. It was a dark, showery day and we did little but sit about camp, eat, and bring our log books up to date.

The next morning we left the sea early and climbed back up the glacier to the dump at the bottom of the cliff. There were nine loads left there. We took six down with us that afternoon and managed to get to the ford of the stream so early that the torrent of water hadn't yet started. These glacier streams flow much more rapidly in the late afternoon, when the sun is melting the ice fast, than they do earlier in the day.

A short wade, only knee deep this trip, and we were back at camp with only three loads left to get. Dick and I had a big job of mapping and geology the next day, so that we had taken a bit more than our share, while the rest were to go back for the remaining loads, and Art to scout out several miles of the beach toward Lituya Bay.

Behind the Sea Camp, across the creek, rose three queer little pyramid-shaped hills. Ever since I had spotted them in one of the pictures, months before, I'd wanted to poke around on them. There was something wonderful and wild and mysterious about these little mounds of virgin forest nearly surrounded by ice.

When we parted the next morning Dick and I followed the old route to the cliff for about a third of the way up the glacier and then cut off to the left towards the base of the southernmost and highest of the hills. The glacier flows right up against the back of them and, split in two by their knife-like action, runs on one side of them toward our camp and on the other toward Cape Fairweather, three miles to the west of camp up the beach.

The side of the hill that faces the glacier is all bare rock and gravel, where the ice has worn the trees away. On the other side,

Loading on a Ninety-Five-Pound Pack at the Sea Camp.

facing the sea, is the most beautiful virgin forest that could possibly be imagined.

Apparently the easiest way to get to the top of the first hill was to get behind it on the glacier and then go up that gravel slope. So we crossed the rolling, hilly ice to the place where it divided behind the hills and scrambled up the steep gravel slope to the top of Number One, as we called it.

A beautiful, mossy bear trail led on toward the notch between One and Two and we followed this till it suddenly stopped in a fierce thicket of devil's club that led down a steep pitch to the notch. A pair of tiny fresh-water ponds were situated exactly in the notch and we had a mighty hard fight through the devil's club and undergrowth to get past them and onto the ridge of Number Two.

Halfway down the slope I heard a muffled crash in the bushes ahead of us. We had left the bear trail but a moment before and I stopped stock still, listening. We didn't move a twig for what seemed a fearfully long time. Then we decided that it was nothing but a scare and started on again. In a second the same sound was repeated, but this time we solved the riddle—it was nothing but a rock I had loosened with my feet that had fallen into the brook-bed below us.

What a relief! We made the notch in only about ten minutes all the way from the top of One and a ten minute climb up another animal trail on the ridge of Two brought us to its top. The hills were *much* smaller than they had looked from below. We'd expected to spend all day climbing them and here we were only two hours out of camp and already on top of the second.

A beautiful carpet of moss covered the summit of the hill and, sitting on it, we had lunch leaning against two ninety-foot fir trees. It was as near a perfect day as we had had all summer. Only here and there a light cloud drifted along over the Coast Range. Fairweather reared herself up in tremendous, ever-changing vistas as we saw her through the trees and those floating mists.

A much deeper notch than the one which we had just passed separated the last two hills from each other. It took a good twenty minutes even to get down into it and when we got there the sight of another pond, this time a good two hundred yards across, was too much for us to stand.

A fine sunny beach dropped steeply into the icy glacier water. In scarcely a minute we were both ready for a swim.

I asked Dick to snap a picture of me diving in, but it took me so long to make up my mind and gather up my nerve for the frigid plunge that he got one of me standing on the beach ready for a dive, but still undecided as to whether or not it should be made!

For a half hour geology, mapping, hills—everything was forgotten in a series of dips and sun baths. It was two in the afternoon before we started up the last hill, still following our bear trail and whistling loudly as we went.

From the top of Number Three the view over Cape Fairweather and the big ponds at the end of the Plateau Glacier was every bit worth the trouble of climbing the hill. The view to the south down the coast toward Lituya Bay, too, was grand.

Instead of our geology hammer, we'd brought along a hatchet with us. Now we climbed a tree a good eighty feet high that stood right on top of the hill and with the hatchet we cleared a big crow's nest in its very top. From there we got pictures in every direction, unhindered by underbrush or the thick growth of big trees.

Our descent down the fifty-degree slope on the far side of the last hill was partially made from alder to alder in monkey fashion, swinging from branch to branch. The last half was steep moraine. We ran down that.

It was still so warm in the sun even at four in the afternoon that we stripped off all our clothes but running pants and hurried back to camp over the ice in that light attire.

In the evening after supper, a light breeze coming off the sea whisked away the flies and mosquitoes and made our driftwood blaze crackle merrily. A crew of six contented fellows sat singing in the firelight in front of the tent until late that night. The loads were off the mountain. The climb was over.

We chatted till the blaze had died to a bed of embers and a full moon had risen over the rolling, sparkling sea. Then we turned in and went to sleep with the lonely tune of the surf ringing in our ears.

CHAPTER XI

BACK TO THE BAY

If it hadn't been for the black flies at the Sea Camp we might have stayed there a bit longer, but by the time that the last load had come down from the cliff we were quite ready to rush through to Lituya Bay in the fastest possible way.

The morning after our Three Hill trip I tried to write my diary outside the hut on an air matress propped up against a log. It was just hopeless. The flies were so thick that it was impossible to try to write or concentrate or even think. They buzzed around our heads in great swarms the second that we left the tent, but they never went inside. However, the tent was so hot inside that it was impossible to exist in it on a sunny day. The flies knew that as well as we did. Outside we swatted continually and every swat floored at least a half a dozen of them.

Fly-fighting had been a luxury at glacier camp weeks before, but it was no longer a novelty. We loaded up ninety pounds each after breakfast and packed it eight miles down the beach—that left six more miles to lug it into the bay.

That night was our last night in camp and we sang and chatted louder and longer than ever before—the bonfire roaring away till nearly midnight. Then in the morning we tore the tent down and rolling it up to the accompaniment of the usual million black flies, we set off down the beach the last time.

Beach-packing, although one can carry a big load as easily as a small one, is a slow, tiring amusement. The hard sand is near the waves, but not in the water, and we found it nearly impossible to keep a straight line near the waves without being swamped occasionally.

Our feet slipped at each step. Our calves grew weary mighty quickly. At last a bear trail was discovered right along the edge of the woods near the beach. A beach looks so flat and inviting it is hardly possible to believe that a bear trail could be better going. But an Alaskan beach with ninety pounds on your back is a different question from a dip at Atlantic City!

We lunched where the loads had been left the day before and passing a dozen deserted log cabins, we came to "Four-Mile-Creek," the place where our pessimistic miner friends said that they were to work till October.

Nothing but a rusty sand-blowing machine and a recently vacated camp site met our eyes. Perhaps we'd find them at the big cabin a mile and a half from the bay. Their Ford tractor-truck had worn out a fine woodroad all the way, and in forty more minutes we were at the cabin.

The miners were gone. Its occupants were two Russians. We managed to make out from their broken English that the miners had left for Juneau three weeks before by boat and had sold them the truck and all of their outfit for $300.00. They must have been hard up for ready money!

We thought little of miners or outfits, however, when John, the elder trapper, produced a pan of red-hot soda biscuits from the oven and set it on the table with a bowl of wild strawberry jam. Bread! It tasted like ambrosia after living six weeks on crackers and biscuits. The jam was made of fresh berries picked just the day before. Then and there we made a big trade. We gave the trappers a small gasoline stove for the use of their car the next day. We'd take the old wreck down to Four-Mile-Creek, pack our gear through to there, and run it in to the bay on the truck.

It's maximum speed was five miles an hour, but little did we care so long as we could walk behind and watch our loads move ahead on something other than our own shoulders.

That night we spent with Bill on the boat. He was a surprised man if I ever saw one when he first caught sight of us. Luckily we had no trouble in finding him, as he was already at the mouth of the bay to pick strawberries for jam—the strawberry crop is at its height in August and all of the clearings and meadows are covered with luscious, big berry patches.

A grand supper and sleep and a tremendous breakfast of flap-jacks and syrup sent us all off the boat next morning with a heart to kill. It was the last load.

At One-and-a-Half-Mile Cabin we got the Ford and then the work began. The radiator leaked. The carburetor leaked. The steering apparatus was broken and it took a man at each front wheel as well as one at the steering wheel to keep the car on the road. Even at best it couldn't have made more than three miles an hour.

Now and then all steering way would be lost and she would crash into a tree, only to be dragged back into the road and started again.

The ride out may have been wild, but the whole homeward journey was the climax of the whole trip. The truck was loaded down with over 500 pounds of our equipment. Gene was a mental as well as physical wreck after driving it out, so Ken took the wheel, John sitting by his side.

A clank of many gears and a deafening roar and we were off. I rushed ahead taking movies. Gene and Batch twisted the wheel. Art worked wherever he was needed.

Dick walked behind talking with Ivan, the other Russian, who told him about his escape from a Soviet prison camp, his race to Vladivostock, and then bumming his way across the Bering Straits to Alaska. He was a wild-looking fellow with a long double-edged hunting knife at his belt and a great rifle slung across his shoulders.

Part way back to camp John took the wheel of his car and immediately drove it full speed into a tree and stalled it. After a little while he managed to learn enough to keep the machine on the road, but as for stopping it—he had no idea what to do in an emergency and merely pushed and pulled everything in sight, steering into the bushes while he did so.

A wide stream had to be forded just before we reached the trappers' cabin. Ken took over the controls there and, bouncing, jolting, and splashing, he guided the machine across and safely to a stop on the other side.

A cup of coffee all around. We had been laughing so hard steadily for two hours that we needed it badly. Then we were off again. Those last one and a half miles were terrific. Only ten minutes from the cabin the leaves of the front spring began to disintegrate and the steering rod became twisted into a perfect corkscrew.

Right then and there we got rocks and an iron bar, and assisted by three prospectors who were staying on the island with Jim, we smashed the spring back together again, tied it in place, and bent the steering rod as straight as a rock could do it (not very straight).

At seven in the evening, after eight steady hours on the "trail," the Lituya Bay Transportation Company, as we now called ourselves, dumped its load on the beach and piled it aboard the boat. Two days later, some equipment that we had left had been brought down from Camp II, and we were headed out of the bay by Cormorant Rock. The old tide rip, now passed at the right time, didn't give us its usual scare. We sailed slowly down the coast at first in a light rain and then under dark skies. A sou'wester was again on the way for us and we must make Cape Spencer.

At nine that night, eight hours after leaving the bay, we cleared the light and started down Cross Sound, bound for Juneau once more.

The trip back seemed to last but a second compared with those long days of waiting at Soapstone in June. And then came telegrams and packing and a midnight boat for the south with baths and beds and clean clothes and fresh milk and cream.

But there isn't a one of us who wouldn't give a fortune to be back again in the shadow of old Fairweather packing in the rain, sleeping on the ice, eating bran-flakes and water, and playing hide-and-seek with the bears.

FOOD LISTS

CONTENTS of FOOD BAGS

SPECIAL MISCELLANEOUS
Butter in odd bags through number 43 and in all bags thereafter.
Klim in every other odd bag.
Brown sugar in odd bags above number 20.
Cocoa in bags above number 30.
A dish towel in every bag.
Brillo (steel wool) in every bag.
Can opener in every odd bag.

DAILY MENUS
ODD BAGS BELOW NUMBER 20
Compote of Apricots and Apples
Eggs and Bacon
Oatmeal, Coffee
2 boxes Sardines
1 box Vegetized Wafers
Dried Apricots
Chocolate, Life Savers
Mouquin Chicken cubes (12)
Rice
Canned Tongue (in bags No. 1, 5, 9, 13, 17)
Corned Beef Hash (in bags No. 3, 7, 11, 15, 19)

Carrots
Edgemont Crackers, Marmalade
Butter
Klim (in bags No. 1, 5, 9, 13, 17)
Brillo, can opener, towel

EVEN BAGS BELOW NUMBER 21
Prunes
Eggs and Bacon
Cornmeal
Coffee
Cheese
Vegetized wafers
Figs
Chocolate, Fruit drops
Vegex (12)
Roast Beef
Macaroni
Corn
Brown Bread
Dates
Sugar
Towel

ODD BAGS NUMBERS 21–29
Prunes, hot cereal and milk
Coffee

Sardines (2 boxes)
Vegetized wafers
Apricots
Chocolate, Life Savers
Vegex,
Roast beef
Potatoes
Brown bread
Pecans
Sugar
Brown sugar
Klim (in bags No. 21, 25, 29)
Butter
Brillo, can opener, towel

EVEN BAGS NUMBERS 22–30
Prunes
Eggs and bacon
Coffee
Cheese
Vegetized wafers
Chocolate
Figs
Fruit drops
Beef cubes
Chicken (2 cans)
Potatoes
Edgemont crackers
Jam, sugar
Towel

ODD BAGS NUMBERS 31–49
INCLUSIVE
Prunes
Hot cereal and milk
Coffee
Cheese
Vegetized wafers

Raisins, apricots
Chocolate, fruit drops
Vegex
Roast beef
Potatoes
Spinach
Brown bread
Pecans
White sugar, brown sugar,
Klim (in bags No. 33, 37, 41, 45,
    49)
Cocoa (in bags No. 41, 43,
    45, 47)
Butter,
Brillo, can opener, towel

EVEN BAGS NUMBERS 32–50
INCLUSIVE
Prunes
Eggs and bacon
Coffee
Cheese
Vegetized Wafers
Raisins, apricots
Chocolate, fruit drops
Beef cubes
Chicken (2 cans)
Potatoes
Spinach
Edgemont crackers
Jam (strawberry)
Sugar
Butter
Towel

PHOTOGRAPH INDEX

The photographs in *Washburn: Extraordinary Adventures of a Young Mountaineer* are a selection of those that were published in the original three Boys' Books by Boys. All of the photographs in this volume's *Among the Alps with Bradford* and *Bradford on Mount Fairweather*, as well as many of Brad Washburn's later photographic works, including the image of Mt. Fairweather that appears on the cover of this book, are available from Panopticon Gallery in Waltham, Massachusetts. For more information, contact Panopticon Gallery at 781-647-0100, or visit its web site: www.panopt.com. For reference, the photographs' negative numbers and/or album locations are listed below.

Bradford on Mount Fairweather

INDEX